MY

HYGGE
HOME

MY
HYGGE
HOME

HOW TO MAKE HOME
YOUR HAPPY PLACE

MEIK WIKING,

CEO, THE HAPPINESS RESEARCH INSTITUTE

PENGUIN LIFE

AN IMPRINT OF

PENGUIN BOOKS

PENGUIN LIFE

UK | USA | Canada | Ireland | Australia
India | New Zealand | South Africa

Penguin Life is part of the Penguin Random House group of companies whose
addresses can be found at global.penguinrandomhouse.com.

First published 2022
001

Copyright © Meik Wiking, 2022

The moral right of the author has been asserted

Colour origination by Altaimage, London
Printed and bound in Italy by Printer Trento

The authorized representative in the EEA is Penguin Random House Ireland,
Morrison Chambers, 32 Nassau Street, Dublin DO2 YH68

A CIP catalogue record for this book is available from the British Library

ISBN: 978–0–241–51797–0

www.greenpenguin.co.uk

Contents

———

CHAPTER

1

—

DANISH DESIGN
AND HYGGE
HEADQUARTERS

Can our homes make us happier? Can we design for wellbeing? Can we create better homes where we not only live, but thrive? The answers to these questions had been under my nose all the time. Because growing up in Denmark means you grow up with two things. Design and hygge.

You may be familiar with some of the names of Danish designers. Arne Jacobsen, Hans Wegner, Poul Kjærholm, Poul Henningsen and Børge Mogensen are not just Danish household names, they are design icons throughout the world – and if you have watched Danish TV dramas such as *Borgen*, *The Killing* and *The Legacy*, you have had a glimpse of Danish urban and interior design.

In fact, you may be one of those people who pause *Borgen* just to make sure those were Poul Henningsen Artichoke lamps in the prime minister's office. That attention to detail is why these shows have sometimes been referred to as 'furniture porn'. By the way, I googled 'furniture porn'. Regretted it immediately. Not what I thought!

Artichoke Lamp designed by Poul Henningsen in 1925

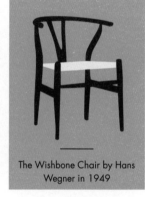

The Wishbone Chair by Hans Wegner in 1949

Bølling Tray Table designed by Hans Bølling in 1963

Denmark is so linked with design that when the Simpsons – in the cartoon show – go to Denmark, the flight attendant instructs the passengers to apply the final coat of varnish if they have been designing and building furniture during the flight.

But design goes beyond beautiful chairs. Design by its very definition is a plan to show the function or workings of a place or an object before it is created. It is to imagine how a place or a thing could be different and how this difference may impact on us.

Design impacts on how we move in our cities, what food we put on our plate, how we interact with our loved ones, whether we have dinner with our neighbours, how happy we are at work and what we do with the time that we have been given. In short, it impacts on the fabric of life and what makes life worth living.

Design can inspire us to become better human beings, to change the world positively, and if we harness the power of design, we have the tools to improve our quality of life.

That was the foundation of Danish design. It's a design tradition with a humanistic approach. Design for human beings. An ambition to create functional products with superior quality for the ordinary citizen. Products that could be bought by the average worker. A combination of simplicity, functionality, sustainability, quality, user-friendliness and aesthetics. And design in Denmark has always been a broad field. Architecture, for instance, has always been a big part of it; architects would typically not only design the building but everything in it – furniture that fitted the building and cutlery that fitted the restaurant.

One example is the SAS Hotel in the centre of Copenhagen, designed from inside to out by Arne Jacobsen in 1960.

Danish design is all about making where we live the best possible environment for our health and wellbeing. Or as John Heskett, professor at the Institute of Design at Illinois Institute of Technology and School of Design at Hong Kong Polytechnic University, puts it, 'Design, stripped to its essence, can be defined as the human capacity to shape and make our environment in ways without precedent in nature, to serve our needs and give meaning to our lives.' Perhaps there is only one thing bigger than design in Denmark – and that is hygge.

The importance of hygge

——

Hygge is the art of creating a nice atmosphere. It is about being with the people we love. A feeling that we are safe, that we are shielded from the world and can allow ourselves to let our guard down. You may be having an endless conversation about the small or big things in life – or just be comfortable in each other's silent company – or you may simply just be by yourself, enjoying a cup of tea. It is the feeling of home. In other words, hygge is about how we turn a house into a home – into a place where we find comfort and connection. Designing your hygge home is to imagine which activities can take place here that will have a positive impact on your wellbeing – and then shaping your living space to make that happen.

It's difficult to overstate how important hygge is to the Danes and the Danish culture. The Danish obsession with hygge seems so ingrained in our cultural DNA and national values that to say you don't care about it would be as much of a social faux pas in Denmark as it would be for a British person to say, 'I don't think we should stay calm – I think we should freak out' or an American saying, 'I've been thinking lately about this freedom thing – and I've come to the conclusion that it is not for me.' Let me try to demonstrate just how much hygge means to us.

In 2016, the Danish Minister for Culture asked the Danish people the following question: Which social values, traditions or movements that have shaped us in Denmark will you carry through to tomorrow's society? It was part a national quest to uncover which values have made Danes who we are and would shape society in the future – a Denmark canon. They received more than two thousand suggestions and the ten most important ones were decided upon by the ministry. They included the welfare state, freedom, trust, equality and yes – you guessed it – hygge.

In 2019, when the International Astronomical Union celebrated its hundredth anniversary, it awarded each country a planet and asked them to name it. In Denmark, of the 830 suggestions sent in, five were chosen as possibles – hygge was one of them. (Muspelheim won, the name of the burning heat that comes from the south and is guarded by Surt, the fire giant, in Norse mythology. Admittedly, slightly cooler than chocolate by candlelight.)

In Denmark, you can even write your Ph.D. on hygge. The first to do this was Jeppe Linnet, and no, it does not mean he spent three years researching the perfect number of cinnamon buns to eat in a day (he discovered that after six months). In fact, Jeppe conducted extensive ethnographic research on how Danes related to their home and how hygge influences the consumption of hospitality, food and drinks. According to his findings, hygge is a situational sense of ease and pleasure – enjoying the here and now – an atmosphere that consists in the way you are with people, the mood of the encounter and the feel of the physical space. The surroundings are very important when it comes to the feeling of hygge. It is about places with atmosphere.

Homes are hygge headquarters to the Danes. Not only is it where we relax and recharge, home is also central to our social life in Denmark. Whereas

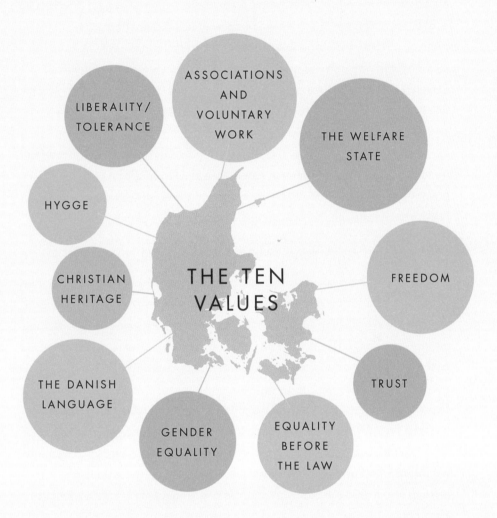

ASSOCIATIONS AND VOLUNTARY WORK

LIBERALITY/ TOLERANCE

THE WELFARE STATE

HYGGE

FREEDOM

CHRISTIAN HERITAGE

THE TEN VALUES

THE DANISH LANGUAGE

TRUST

GENDER EQUALITY

EQUALITY BEFORE THE LAW

other countries have a culture of socializing predominantly in bars, restaurants and cafés, Danes prefer *hjemmehygge* (home hygge). Perhaps it is because going out in Denmark is relatively expensive or because Danes are typically introverted people and feel more comfortable in their own surroundings. You can easily tell an introverted Dane from an extroverted Dane. The introverted Dane will look at their shoes and the extroverted Dane will look at your shoes. We are a nation of silent Northmen and -women.

Combined with our passion for design, this makes us a nation of introverted nesters with hygge as a national sport. So when Covid-19 hit and the government asked Danes to stay away from crowds, stay indoors, spend time in our homes with as few people as possible, we Danes were, like, 'We've got this. We've been practising for this our entire lives!'

But, recently, hygge has also become a global phenomenon. Every year, the World Happiness Report presents a list of happiness levels around the world. The five Nordic countries – Denmark, Sweden, Norway, Finland and Iceland – usually top the rankings. That has led to increasing interest in the culture and way of life of Scandinavian countries – such as Danish hygge.

Search for books on hygge on Amazon and you'll get more than five hundred results. I wrote one of them. It has been translated into more than thirty-five languages and has sold over a million copies. It set sail in Denmark but has reached every global shore. It has become the second Viking invasion – but this time the hygge hordes are armed with blankets and hot chocolate.

Obviously, even before the spread of the word 'hygge', Danes were not the only ones who could enjoy the pleasure that comes from being in good company, in front of the fire, with some mulled wine. As Shakespeare famously wrote in *Romeo and Juliet*, 'What's in a name? That which we call a rose/ By any other name would smell as sweet.' Denmark does not have a monopoly on hygge.

I often think of a letter I received after I first wrote about hygge. It was from a French woman, a mother of two young kids, who had been familiar with the feeling of hygge but had not been able to put it into words before now. 'I have had hygge all my life,' she wrote, 'I just didn't know there was a word for that feeling. Before now I would have spent an afternoon with my two kids. We could have been on the sofa with some tea and some biscuits and spent the entire afternoon there. Earlier, I would have called that a lazy afternoon. Now I call that a hygge afternoon.' That made me happy. With the introduction of a word, a concept, a feeling, we had removed the element of guilt from what should be a perfectly fine way to spend an afternoon – making your kids feel loved and comforted. A rose may smell as sweet by any other name – but hygge just feels better.

It is a great pleasure for me to see how many people have embraced hygge. I think we could all use more togetherness, warmth, relaxation and simple pleasures in our lives. That is not a Danish thing. That is a human thing. And I think we all deserve to have a hygge home that offers us a place to be happy, even in times of turbulence. In our own little worlds, we are masters of the universe. And maybe finding happiness at home will make us better equipped to make the world a better place.

Hygge and happiness

——

Fortunately, the capacity of hygge to bring people together seems universal across cultures and geographical borders. And sometimes, we need do no more than light a candle to create a sense of hygge around our dinner tables.

'After I read about *hygge* I went out and bought two candelabras and we started lighting them at dinner,' one of my readers told me. He and his wife have three sons: eighteen-year-old twins and a son who was fifteen at the time. When he first started to light candles for dinner his boys teased him. 'What's with the romance, Dad? Do you want to have dinner alone with Mum?' But soon he noticed small changes around the dinner table. Time seemed to slow down. The teenagers became more talkative. The change in atmosphere at the table put the boys in storytelling mood. 'They don't just shovel in the food any more, they sip their wine, they tell us about their day.' By making this simple change, dinnertime is no longer just about food – it is about hygge. And now the boys are the ones who light the candles for dinner.

A small design change had a big impact. A different dinner set-up changed how a family interacted. More hygge led to longer family dinners. That got me thinking. If a small change like a candle could have such a large effect, what other hygge design hacks could have a positive impact on our

happiness? How do we create spaces and places that have an impact on our wellbeing? How do we improve our quality of life through architecture, lighting, decor and furniture? Can we design for happiness?

Perhaps you have experienced how the atmosphere in a room can impact your mood. Perhaps you've also experienced the feeling of walking into a place and wanting to stay there. Maybe it was the warmth of the sunlight coming through the windows or maybe the shelves of books you wanted to explore, or maybe it just felt like home.

My job is to understand why you felt that way. I study happiness and how we can improve our wellbeing. A decade ago, I set up the Happiness Research Institute in Copenhagen. I know, the Happiness Research Institute sounds like a magical place. People imagine all we do all day is play with puppies and balloons and eat ice cream. Sorry to burst your bubble – but we only do that on Wednesdays. In reality, we use scientific methods to understand happiness. We undertake studies over several years and use massive data sets and ask why some people are happier than others.

For the past ten years, the Happiness Research Institute has examined how spaces and places impact on our wellbeing, and I have become increasingly curious about the connection between our homes and our happiness, and more and more aware of the relationship between our environment and our emotions.

My curiosity has been driven by both professional and personal reasons. At the institute my colleagues and I are always trying to answer questions, based on the happiness data that we receive, for example, how should we design our societies, our cities, our offices, our homes and our lives differently? It's incredible how much our research can tell us about how to best use the space around us, and that's what I'm going to share with you in this book.

As I was analysing this research I was also looking to improve my own personal quality of life by finding a new place to live. In my life I have lived in twenty different places. There was the place where I loved how the light fell through the windows, and there was the room I had with no windows. There was my apartment in a small Spanish town, and there was my apartment in Mexico's second-biggest city. There was the apartment I lived in after a bad break-up, with a mattress and a TV on the floor (I called the design 'Scandinavian minimalism on steroids'), and there is the tiny place I have on the island of Bornholm, where you can see the ocean and you know that everything is going to be OK.

But when the Covid-19 pandemic first hit, my girlfriend and I found ourselves in a small apartment with no balcony. Fun! So one morning I woke up very grumpy. (Happiness researchers are people too, you know.) It was before my morning coffee, and more bad news was hitting the headlines. Corona cases were on the rise – and to make matters worse, a new strain had jumped from mink to humans in Denmark which could take the world back to step one in the search for an effective vaccine.

Like millions of people, my life and my work were affected by the pandemic. The Happiness Research Institute works globally, and never had so many planes been on the ground and so many things up in the air, making it difficult to conduct studies as normal – developing ideas on how to improve quality of life for a small town in Austria is difficult when you cannot leave Denmark. Furthermore, our new Happiness Museum had opened its doors for the first time to an empty Copenhagen. Personally, I missed seeing friends and family. And I missed not worrying about – well – everything.

So that morning, I was mid-rant about minks and mutations when my girlfriend cut me off. 'You cannot control virus mutations. Focus on what you can control.' We may not always have control over the events affecting us, but we always have control over how we approach things. And while we may live in a turbulent world, we can still make our homes a happy place. That evening we did have the power to create a nice candlelit dinner with our favourite food and a meaningful and fun conversation, and I quickly forgot all about my morning rant.

Safe space

———

Our homes are zones of control and where we find comfort and safety.
Our homes are where we connect with loved ones and let our guard down.
Our homes are where we re-energize to take on the world once more.
In a world that sometimes seems to be becoming increasingly turbulent and
chaotic, demanding more and more of our attention and becoming ever
more stressful, our homes are where we can retreat to and seek refuge.
Maybe that is why our language is lined up with love for the home. There is
no place like home. Home sweet home. Home is where the heart is. Or,
according to Laura Ingalls Wilder, author of the *Little House on the Prairie*
books – 'home' is the nicest word there is.

Even before Covid-19, we had become the indoor species. Some studies
suggest we spend around 90 per cent of our time indoors, and we spend
more time than anywhere else in our homes. The National Human Activity
Pattern Survey looked at where 9,386 Americans spent their time between
1992 and 1994 (see p. 28). And spending time at home has only become
more common since. We work, we sleep, we cook, we watch television, we
clean, we do homework, and we throw dinner parties at home. This is where
the majority of our lives play out. But how our homes impact on our
wellbeing remains relatively unexplored.

WHERE WE SPEND OUR TIME

68.7%
Residence

5.5%
In a vehicle

11%
Other indoor location

1.8%
Bar/restaurant

5.4%
Office/factory

7.6%
Outdoors

Most research to date has focused on the physical health effects of the design and construction of our built environment. However, in recent years there has been more recognition of the importance of our mental and social health, and the awareness that how we design and build our environment impacts on how we feel and interact with other people is growing.

Most people prefer natural to artificial light. We prefer having a window by our workspace. We prefer a view of trees over bricks. These preferences aren't just aesthetic, they are directly linked to our mental health. One large study into European housing and health status by the World Health Organization suggested that inadequate daylight or unattractive window views increased the likelihood of depression in inhabitants by 60 per cent and 40 per cent respectively. But design of the built environment rarely focuses on these design elements to improve mental health.

Fortunately, we are currently witnessing a return to the definition of health given by the World Health Organization in 1948: 'Health is a state of complete physical, mental and social wellbeing and not merely the absence of disease or infirmity.' Our homes, our workplaces and our cities should be places that ensure not only our physical health and wellbeing but – equally importantly – our mental and social wellbeing. So, what if we could build not only a shelter to keep us physically safe but also one that helps us flourish mentally and socially? What if we, through having more nurturing and happy homes, could foster more meaningful conversations and stronger relationships?

One of the things I have realized is that we look for happiness in so many places, but perhaps we have been looking for happiness in the wrong places. Perhaps happiness is actually closer to home than we think.

In 2018, the Happiness Research Institute partnered up with Kingfisher (owner of B&Q, Screwfix and other DIY stores throughout Europe) in an effort to understand what makes a happy home. We surveyed 13,480 people from ten different countries, asking them how happy they are in general and how happy they are with their homes. The chart opposite shows how much certain factors impacted on their overall happiness.

We found that 73 per cent of the people who feel happy about their home also feel happy in general but, more importantly, that 15 per cent of people's overall happiness could be explained by their home or their satisfaction with it. Fifteen per cent may not sound like a lot – but think of how many factors have an impact on your happiness. Your relationships (married people are on average happier), your health (especially your mental health), your job (a sense of meaning and purpose is key), your age (it is U-shaped – you are likely to be least happy in your mid-forties), and so on. With so many factors impacting on our happiness, it actually takes a lot to move the needle – so 15 per cent is a sizeable chunk.

Another study, conducted by Realdania, one of the biggest foundations in Denmark, with a mission to improve the quality of life through the built environment, found that only 7.5 per cent of people say their home has no or very little influence on their quality of life. The study also showed that it becomes even more important to people the older they become.

We need to embrace the idea that spaces and places definitely can have a positive impact on our wellbeing. That we can improve our quality of life through changing the spaces around us – and, therefore, that we can design for happiness. Or, to paraphrase Winston Churchill, we shape our homes and then they shape us. They affect how we feel and how we act.

WHAT HAS THE GREATEST IMPACT ON YOUR HAPPINESS?

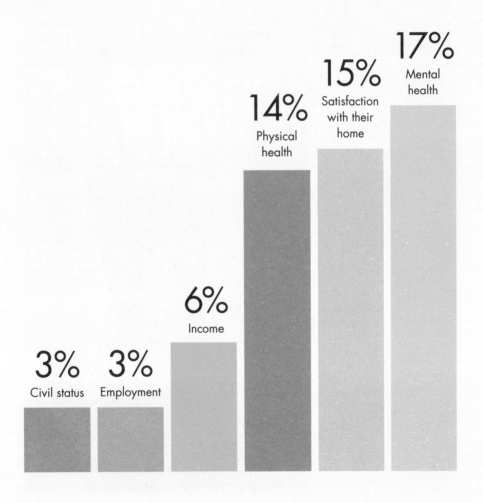

3%
Civil status

3%
Employment

6%
Income

14%
Physical health

15%
Satisfaction with their home

17%
Mental health

THE ARCHITECTURE OF
HAPPINESS CHECKLIST

———

❑ Start observing how different places make you feel. What is it about a space that makes you feel relaxed and at home? Consider what you could take from it to make your space feel the same.

❑ Consider how much time you spend in different locations and how the design and decor of those places impact on your behaviour.

❑ Remember that small design changes can have a big impact. Switch the lamps around or try out candles during dinner. There is nothing wrong with starting small.

CHAPTER

2

—

HYGGE,
A PERFECT
NIGHT IN

It is said that in Denmark there are thirteen months in a year. January, February, March, April, May, June, July, August, September, October, November, November and December.

Right now it is November in Copenhagen. That means it is windy, dark and wet. Basically, the triathlon of lousy weather. Drops of rain are hitting hard against the windows and you can sense the wind wrestling with the building. Soup is simmering in the kitchen and I can smell that the bread in the oven will soon be done. I check the weather forecast, and the rain and wind are likely to last a day or two. I open the fridge and see there is no need to visit the supermarket for the next couple of days. I have the evening to myself, but Nina Simone is keeping me company, and we are both feeling good. Perhaps Jane Austen said it best: There is nothing like staying at home for real comfort.

Hygge is circling the wagons around the campfire. It is finding comfort in our shelter when the storm is raging or when winter has come. Perhaps that is why some people may be in greater need of a hygge home than others.

Hygge – a northern state of mind?

___

Interestingly, if you look at which of the US states google 'hygge' the most, a pattern emerges. The top five are all northern states: Vermont, Minnesota, Maine, Oregon and Washington, while the bottom five are the southern states of Mississippi, Louisiana, Alabama, Hawaii and Florida.

The same pattern can be seen among countries. Denmark, Finland and Norway google 'hygge' the most and Mexico, Indonesia and India the least.

So maybe being far from the equator brings you closer to hygge – or perhaps more in need of hygge. Maybe those cold, dark winter months drive us to hygge hibernation. When the darkness descends we seek shelter indoors, we light the candles, bring out the blankets and let the comfort food simmer on the stove. Perhaps hygge is a Nordic necessity, or at least a northern state of mind.

So what do Danes know about the state of Vermont? Two things. Cheddar cheese and Ben and Jerry's Ice Cream. All sounds very hygge to me. I see a new licence-plate slogan. Vermont – the hygge state.

RATE OF GOOGLE SEARCHES FOR 'HYGGE' IN US STATES

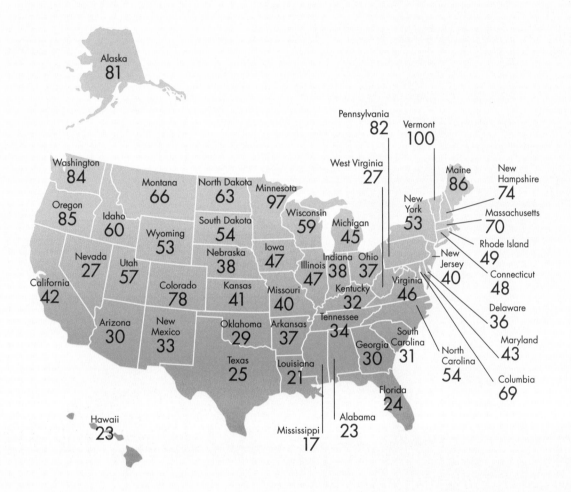

Alaska 81

Pennsylvania 82
Vermont 100
West Virginia 27
Maine 86
New Hampshire 74

Washington 84
Montana 66
North Dakota 63
Minnesota 97
New York 53
Massachusetts 70

Oregon 85
Idaho 60
South Dakota 54
Wisconsin 59
Michigan 45
Rhode Island 49

Wyoming 53
Nebraska 38
Iowa 47
Indiana 38
Ohio 37
Connecticut 48

Nevada 27
Utah 57
Illinois 47
New Jersey 40

California 42
Colorado 78
Kansas 41
Missouri 40
Kentucky 32
Virginia 46
Delaware 36

Arizona 30
New Mexico 33
Oklahoma 29
Arkansas 37
Tennessee 34
South Carolina 31
Maryland 43

Texas 25
Louisiana 21
Georgia 30
North Carolina 54
Columbia 69

Hawaii 23
Mississippi 17
Alabama 23
Florida 24

The values are shown on a scale of 0 to 100. The higher the number, the more popular the Google search rate for hygge is in that state.

Finding shelter in turbulent times

———

Hygge is something all Danes grow up with; it is part of our everyday language. My good friends Christian and Mette's daughter Ingrid is proof of that. One day, at the age of a year and a half, Ingrid was sitting inside a small playhouse with a teacup and a plate full of sand (when you are eighteen months old, it's delicious, sand is basically caviar for toddlers). She looked up at her parents and said, 'Vi hygger.' We are hygging. 'Hygger.' She repeated and tasted the word. Obviously, the hygge is strong with this one, I thought, and I found it interesting Ingrid had first used the word 'hygge' sitting inside a playhouse. Ingrid is not alone in considering shelter to be part of the hygge home.

A couple of years ago the Happiness Research Institute looked into what role people's home played in their happiness and conducted in-depth interviews with fifty people across Europe, asking them to show us around their homes. We also asked them what they associated the word 'home' with. A clear pattern emerged from the interviews. Whether we were talking with Jane in her forties living in the countryside in North Wales, or Alina, a Russian in her twenties living in Moscow, or Juan in his late sixties living in Jaraíz de la Vera in Spain, they echoed each other's words.

'HOME IS OUR SHELTER. HOME IS OUR PLACE OF REFUGE. HOME IS OUR SANCTUARY. IT IS BASE CAMP – A SAFE HAVEN – A PLACE TO RECHARGE.'

'HOME IS WHERE YOU GO AND EVERYTHING IS OK. IT IS SOMEWHERE YOU CAN CLOSE THE DOOR AND SHUT THE WORLD OUT, WHERE WE ALL ARE SAFE, I SUPPOSE.'

'HOME IS THE BASE; IT IS WHERE YOU RAISE YOUR FAMILY. IT IS A PLACE TO GO AS A REFUGE.'

'IT IS A RETREAT FROM WORK, SOMEWHERE I CAN RELAX AND SWITCH OFF.'

'HOME IS SOMEWHERE I FEEL SAFE AND WARM AND COMFORTABLE. IT IS NICE TO COME BACK TO. IT IS SOMEWHERE WHERE THINGS ARE FAMILIAR.'

'HOME IS A REFUGE, MY CASTLE. I FEEL SAFE, I FEEL PROTECTED, AND I DON'T FEEL IN DANGER, I DON'T FEEL THAT ANYBODY IS GOING TO COME AND BOTHER ME. WITHIN THESE WALLS, I FEEL SAFE.'

This would not have surprised Abraham Maslow, the Russian-American psychologist who in 1943 developed a model demonstrating the pyramid of human needs and argued that life satisfaction depended on meeting these needs. Our homes would have a pride of place in Maslow's belief system.

Our homes help us to meet our primary physiological needs of safety and shelter. Our homes keep us warm and allow us to sleep in peace – the very foundation of our needs. In the chapters to come we will explore how our homes can play a part in meeting the higher needs of the pyramid, from connecting with other people to becoming who we dream of becoming.

But even within the home there are some places that seem to offer a greater sense of shelter and comfort.

THE PYRAMID OF HUMAN NEEDS

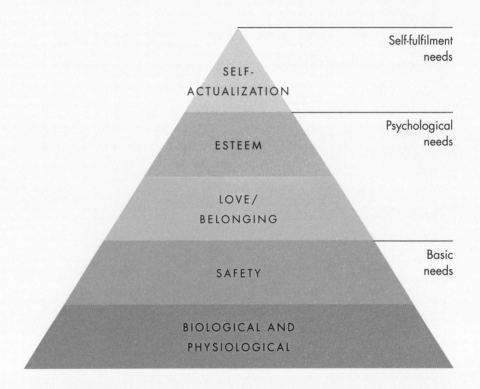

Self-fulfilment
needs

SELF-
ACTUALIZATION

Psychological
needs

ESTEEM

LOVE/
BELONGING

Basic
needs

SAFETY

BIOLOGICAL AND
PHYSIOLOGICAL

Hygge puts baby in the corner

I am writing this sitting in my favourite chair. It is a crisp November morning in Copenhagen, there is a cold, blue sky and the sun is coming through the window to my right. To my left is a green sofa and just behind me a plant and a small shelf of books. I am sitting in the corner of the room, facing three doors, a piano and a dinner table.

I am not sure why I always choose the Viking-proof seat in the house. But I know that I am not the only one who prefers sitting with my back to the wall – and preferably in the corner, so I can observe the whole room. For a lot of people, having the corner just behind you is prime real estate. So the question is, why is this comforting? Why do we like our back to the wall? Is it the feeling of safety or comfort? Perhaps hygge puts baby in the corner.

One theory that could explain our love for nooks is the Prospect–Refuge Theory proposed by English geographer Jay Appleton in *The Experience of Landscape* (1975). The theory proposes that when we examine places to sit or stay we look for qualities that give us the ability to see without being seen. Standing on a hill with a tree behind us would give us both prospect and refuge. Sitting in the mouth of a cave would offer the same benefits – nobody can attack us from behind and we can see what is coming. Maslow placed

the need for safety as the second basic need we seek to fulfil, after shelter.

Imagine that you have an open green space with buildings on all sides. You can sit in the middle of the green space – but there is no cover. Everyone can watch you from their apartments – but you can't see them. Sounds hygge? No, right.

Most of us shy away from sitting in the middle and would choose the edge, but we could instead make the space in the middle better by creating small nooks and pockets. If we added some semicircles of hedges to the large, open green space it would feel nice to sit there. This is why I call my favourite chair Viking-proof. I know there's no danger of any angry invaders sneaking up behind me while I'm working – not that they would, but it's a human instinct to protect ourselves.

No matter what the reason is, the takeaway is to make sure to design places for refuge. To focus. To re-energize. Introvert or not. So when we are creating hygge spaces I think it is important to make sure that we have our Viking-proof places. That goes for your living room – especially if you have a large open-plan space – it goes for the kids' bedrooms, and it goes for the garden, if you have one. Create caves and nooks for us introverts to hang out in with our book and our cup of coffee.

One important learning point is to take from life outside our homes to improve life inside our homes. Let's visit some of my personal heroes.

The hygge scale

—

He was an architect; she was a psychologist. No, it is not the start of an Avril Lavigne song, it's the story of how a couple developed the humancentric approach to architecture and changed Copenhagen for ever.

I still remember the first time I met Jan Gehl. 'It was my wife, Ingrid,' he said. (Note: not all girls in Denmark are called Ingrid.) 'She started asking questions – she is a psychologist. She was more interested in people than in bricks.' And she was suspicious about what was going on in architecture.

'Why are you architects not interested in people? Why don't they teach you anything about people at the school of architecture? Why don't you and your fellow architects ask yourselves, how does the way we shape the buildings impact on how people feel?' That simple question sparked a career that has now lasted more than sixty years as a pioneer in creating liveable cities around the world. How can we design cities that would make people happier simply by living out their daily lives in them?

When Jan graduated from the School of Architecture at the Royal Danish Academy of Fine Arts in 1960, the modernistic movement was in vogue. It was a system-oriented thinking where areas were separated: there were commercial quarters, living quarters, industrial quarters, cultural quarters.

Cities were designed by looking at them from above. This was a time when architects would photograph houses early in the morning – so no people could be seen in the picture and cause a distraction for the observer of the beautiful form they had created.

The same year Jan graduated, Brasilia – Brazil's new capital – was inaugurated. It had been designed from scratch from a viewpoint high above the city – the design looks like a bird – around an axis, to give a sense of monumentality. Beautiful, perhaps – but was it liveable? Not according to Jan – he calls it 'birdshit architecture'. These were streets designed for cars, not people. No one was asking what it would be like to live and commute in a city where everyone was living in the same area and working in the same area across town. No one was asking how it would feel to be less than two metres tall in a city of monumentality.

There was a gap between social science and architecture, and this gap still exists. But in 1965 Jan and Ingrid went on a six-month study trip to Italy and explored how public life unfolded in public spaces. How do life and form interact? How does the way we shape our cities influence our behaviour and our quality of life?

Jan and Ingrid studied how people were using their urban space in some of the oldest streets and most famous squares in the world. Streets that were designed for feet, not wheels, and squares that were designed not from above but for what the human eye can see.

They registered where people walked, and where they would they sit and watch the world go by. Why is it that a certain bench was always the first to be occupied? Is it because people like to stay in a corner where they can

observe the whole space? Which elements make the Piazza del Campo in Siena work so well?

It turns out there are similarities across places and spaces where people enjoy spending time. We seek places where we feel protected, not just from crime and traffic but also from the wind and weather. We seek places that offer comfort and connection, where we can sit comfortably and have conversations. We seek places where we find enjoyment in a beautiful view and the caress of the sun or the shade.

And to really understand how people are going to respond to their surroundings we need to ask how these surroundings look from 140 to 160 centimetres above ground. This is the average human eye level, where most people view the world from. It is not how the model looks from above that is important but how it looks from the perspective of the people using the space and living there. Jan calls it the Human Scale.

Now eighty-five, Jan has been working in architecture for more than sixty years, dedicated to improving quality of life by building better spaces between buildings – squares, parks, streets. In Copenhagen, Jan was instrumental in changing the famous Nyhavn from a parking lot into a recreational area, and Strøget from a street for cars to what is now one of the longest pedestrianized streets in the world, projects that have transformed how people enjoy and perceive the city.

In 2000, Jan established Gehl Architects, which advises cities across the world on how to create liveable spaces. Basically, couple therapy for space and people. From Sydney and Shanghai to San Francisco and Sao Paolo, Gehl Architects has been utilizing the Human Scale. 'We use the Danish word for "cuddly" – hygge – and say, let's make it nice and warm and cosy,' said the practice's director, Riccardo Marini, in an interview with the *Guardian* in 2014. 'The hard-nosed among us might turn around and say, "What's that got to do with anything?" . . . Well, it's got a lot to do with making a place good so people will want to stay there.'

The second time I met Jan was in 2009, during the UN Climate Summit in Copenhagen. I had organized a round table at the town hall for city planners and policy-makers to come together to discuss how urban design could help reduce carbon emissions. There were twenty of us there and I had placed four tables together to form a giant rectangle to seat us all. When Jan arrived he took one look at it and said we had to arrange the tables differently. 'We need to sit closer together – we need to be able to hear each other and look each other in the eye. That is the foundation for reaching a consensus today.'

That is when it first occurred to me that we should take some of the principles for life between the buildings and make principles for life inside the buildings. How the building is designed and decorated plays an enormous role in what is happening inside that building – and we must never lose sight of the human scale, whether we are creating life between the buildings or the life we want *inside* the buildings.

Imagine you are sitting in a room that measures 100 square metres. There is a sofa, a chair and a coffee table. In the ceiling in the middle of the room there is one pendant lamp. Other than that, the room is empty. Does it feel hygge? Would you like to spend an afternoon there, perhaps reading a book? Probably not. In a large room scantily furnished, it feels like something is missing. Minimalism on steroids is not hygge.

Had the room been smaller, the furniture could have worked – or if the larger room had been filled with things for the eyes and the senses. With warmth – with texture – with wanderlust and memories of adventures past.

Plants add life. Books offer exploration and contemplation. Rugs and paintings give warmth and texture and transform the sound of voices into the voices secrets are exchanged in by lovers. Replace the uniform light from above with pockets of light that guide you to the best places. The floor lamp by the sofa whispers, 'Grab a book from the shelf and join me.' The green lamp on the wooden desk with the old-school typewriter asks you to come and play. In the corner a globe sends your eyes and your imagination walking. With each element adding hygge points to the place, an afternoon there would be a treat.

No matter how much space you have at home, we can all learn from the human scale. Give your senses things to enjoy and think about how your surroundings are constructed to support how you want to live there.

Remember the scale for small humans

———

One of my favourite things to do as a kid was to build caves. Either in the ground using shovels, or in my room using blankets. I think my mother preferred the second version. A couple of chairs with a big blanket between them became a hygge fort where this cowboy would spend the night.

Jan talks about how the city should be designed from 140–160 centimetres above ground. I think also it is important to remember how something is experienced from the height of a child. So get down on your knees and see how hygge or not the place is from one metre above ground.

That space under the staircase may work as the perfect hygge corner for the kids – especially if they are Harry Potter fans.

Softness adds to the hygge

——

You may be familiar with the fairy tale 'The Princess and the Pea' by Hans Christian Andersen, a fellow Danish writer.

Once upon a time, one stormy night, a young woman drenched by the rain seeks shelter in a prince's castle. She claims to be a princess, and the prince's mother decides to find out if she is telling the truth. To test her, the prince's mother places a pea in the bed the young woman is offered for the night, hiding it under twenty mattresses and twenty feather duvets. In the morning, the guest tells her hosts that she endured a sleepless night, kept awake by something hard in the bed that she is certain has bruised her. With the proof of her bruised back, the princess passes the test for a true princess. The story was first published in 1835; Danish critics disliked it, as the story lacked a moral.

I dislike the story as well, but the criticism was unjust. The story does indeed contain a moral: it's the pillows, stupid. To sleep in comfort, you have to add pillows. It's not rocket hygge. For quality hygge hibernation, you have to add more softness.

For an extra kick of comfort, add softness to your home and create a space where your whole family or a group of your friends can 'cuddle up'. If you can wrap it around you or it is comfy to sit on, it is hygge. This means pillows, blankets and rugs.

In short, ask yourself, if I trip and fall on this, will it cushion my fall? Blankets: yes. Plastic table: no. Furry Viking helmets fall in between.

Pillows are not just for the sofa. You can soften hard seating on chairs or use throw pillows on the floor. When it comes to pillows, think Oprah: You get a pillow! You get a pillow! You get a pillow!

TIP FOR DESIGNING HAPPINESS

in the hygge zone

If you have a large room or a studio apartment, it will be more hygge if you can create a sense of there being several zones. Consider which activities and moods the room needs to cater for and create zones to meet these needs. One for socializing and eating, perhaps; and one for reading and a sense of comfort and shelter. Here are some ideas.

1. Rugs are a great way to create zones in your room – and the easiest – and because of the softness of the fabric you add hygge points to the room.

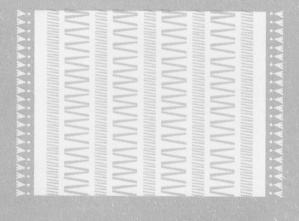

2. Use different lighting in different areas. Don't use a single pendant light from the ceiling in the middle of the room. If you have a dinner table, hang it directly over that, then use floor or table lamps by the sofa or in the lounge area.

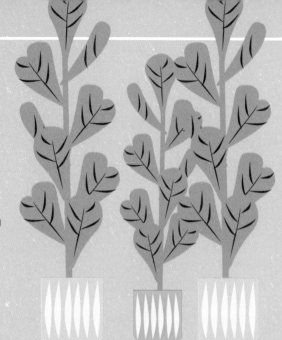

3. Think about adding dividers. Ideally, use ones that allow light to flow through them, for example open shelving. One idea is to use plants, growing them tall to give the sense of a wall you can hygge behind.

4. Create soft seating areas – if you don't have space for a whole sofa but want to create a cosy reading area, beanbags, futons and/or cushions are really effective ways of creating a comfy spot when you need it, while enabling you to be flexible with your space.

5. Use colour to create different moods in different areas. Brighter colours will perk up smaller spaces and are especially useful where there is less natural light.

Be mindful of using the public–private spectrum

———

It is said that Kartoffelrækkerne has the highest concentration of architects in Denmark. *Kartoffelrækkerne* literally means 'the potato rows', and the area takes its name from the potatoes grown there to feed Copenhageners centuries ago – but now, these eleven streets of terraced houses also look like rows of potatoes from above.

I visit one of the streets on a grey day in December. There is no snow, but it is cold and bleak and I have not seen the sun in days. Still, there are kids playing in the street. Two kids are selling imaginary tea from a playhouse. I buy one of the imaginary teas and pay in kind with an imaginary dinosaur called Yggdrasil. Best deal ever.

This is clearly the public part of the built environment. You can walk straight in with your dinosaur. At the other end of the spectrum is inside people's homes. These are the private spaces where people eat and sleep without pushy people trying to sell them tea.

But there are steps between the two extremes along the public–private spectrum. There is a semi-public and semi-private place. For example, people often have a front garden or a front yard. You own the place, and you talk

with your neighbours or nod to people walking by. But every house also has a back yard. You are still as close to the neighbours as you are in the front yards, you can see them and they can see you, but interestingly, there is an unwritten rule that you don't say hi to your neighbours when you see each other in the back yard. You don't talk. I believe this is the difference between semi-public (front yard) and semi-private space (back yard).

I think a hygge home should also provide shelter that offers different types of privacy. Privacy is not only about being alone; it is the opportunity to control access to us. It is not just about separation but, equally, about communication. I believe we all need a place where we can just be ourselves. Yes, we are outside; yes, you can see me; but I just really want to be in my own bubble right now.

Sometimes we're in social mode; sometimes we're in solitude mode. There is a time for interaction and there's a time for introspection. Make sure there is a place you can go to for the different moods you can be in. That goes for inside the home and outside the home.

Stock up on hygge – winter is coming

___

When I was sixteen, I spent a year in a small town in Australia's New South Wales. One of the places I lived was on a farm just outside town. After school, I would help feed the horses and catch runaway sheep, and the evenings were spent in front of the fireplace. Lark Hill was a beautiful farm, and my favourite part of it was the pantry. It was a symphony of pickles and chutneys – jars and cans full of comforting goodness.

On the first page of J. R. R. Tolkien's *The Hobbit*, we learn that a hobbit hole is about comfort and includes a pantry – well, actually, a lot of pantries. The author wrote, 'If more of us valued food and cheer and song above hoarded gold, it would be a merrier world.' I agree. A well-stocked pantry is comforting.

No matter what is going on around us, if there is something to eat at home and a well-stocked pantry, fridge or kitchen cupboard, there is one fail-safe way to hygge hunker down during events beyond our control, whether it's a blizzard or a global pandemic. Hygge is about feeling sheltered from the storm outside – and prepared for the coming of winter. Stocking pantries in our homes is what helped humans (and hobbits) to survive. From earliest times, when there was an abundance of food, humans would preserve the

excess for the winter. We would dry, salt, pickle – make jams, krauts and kimchi. My happy childhood memories smell of elderflowers, as my mother tried to distil summer in a pot.

Today, I spend my summers on the small island of Bornholm, a rock island in the Baltic Sea, and perhaps the most beautiful part of Denmark. Around the house there is a forest full of wild cherries and some great places to pick raspberries, blackberries, figs and apples.

We have spent many evenings picking fruits and berries, and many Sunday afternoons making jams, chutney and the warm cherry sauce for the traditional Christmas dessert in Denmark. Making summer last until Christmas is a pretty good recipe for happiness.

Wood gives warmth several times. When you chop it, when you stack it, when you carry it inside and when you burn it. It is the same with a well-stocked pantry. It gives you comfort and hygge several times: when you grow or forage it, when you cook it, store it and eat it.

Hygge is about enjoying the process. About taking things slowly. And the enjoyment of looking forward to the delicious results you will enjoy tucked up at home on a quiet wintry evening. It's about enriching this time at home by knowing that you've got plenty of delights in store, ready for the perfect hygge moment. It's about making your nights in special, and never feeling that you are missing out.

Stocking up and creating a small pantry also means understanding and respecting the ebb and flow of seasonality in nature. Strawberries do not grow all year round in Denmark. Strawberries in the supermarket midwinter are neither tasty nor hygge. Eating seasonally means a redesign of what we eat when. It means eating or preserving foods that are grown and harvested locally.

Here are my top-ten pantry items:

1. Salted lemons
2. Elderflower cordial
3. Dried mushrooms
4. Rosehip chutney
5. Pickled beetroot

6. Cherry sauce
7. Roasted peppers in oil
8. Kimchi
9. Blackberry jam
10. Figs in rum

TIP FOR DESIGNING HAPPINESS

---

keep a list of your freezer stock on your phone

When you put something in the freezer, you think, 'I can see this is Bolognese and I will know it is Bolognese three months from now.' The thing is, three months from now, you will have added three other containers of brownish leftovers, so it is now very difficult to tell what exactly this frozen lump of brown is and you end up eating spaghetti with duck sauce. Make sure you label your leftovers clearly.

In addition to this, I find it really useful to have an up-to-date list on my phone of what there is in the freezer. It is good to know on an evening when you get home from work later than expected that you have something in the freezer that can be put in a pot, left on the stove and then – voilà! – dinner is ready. Lamb casserole, minestrone soup and duck ragout are just some of my go-tos that have saved me on these occasions.

THE ARCHITECTURE OF
HAPPINESS CHECKLIST

———

❑ Remember that the feeling of shelter comes in different forms, so make sure you have somewhere in your home that gives you that sense of protection. This includes making sure you have a Viking-proof seat.

❑ A hygge home should allow space for privacy and for socialization. Identify and create different steps on the public–private spectrum. Make sure you have places that are suited to your social activities and to quality alone time.

❑ Consider the human scale and think about how you can fill your space with things that make you smile.

❑ Stock up on hygge. Think about how you could make it cosy inside if there were a storm outside. Think, if you were snowed in for three days, what would you choose to have in your pantry?

CHAPTER

3

—

SHINING A
LIGHT ON
HAPPINESS

Sixty something million years ago, the dinosaurs were made suddenly extinct when a large asteroid hit Earth and atmospheric particles blocked the sunlight for several years. Danes calls this period January. Last January, I saw a Danish weather report for the following ten days – not a single chance of sunlight. We don't get a lot of sun in winter. That is why Danes are drawn to a ray of sun like moths are to a flame. I have a scar to prove it.

One morning fifteen years ago I woke up in a country house just outside Siena. I was there for a wedding, got up before the rest of the guests and headed downstairs to the kitchen. I loaded the espresso maker and lit the stove. There was a small square window in the kitchen and through it I could see the brown autumn fields and a clear blue sky. I felt happy and wanted to take a deep breath of the lovely fresh air. I stuck my head out the window, only to discover it was not open and I had put my head through the window, breaking it, waking up everyone in the house. To make matters worse, nobody even nicknamed me Scarface at the wedding. Nevertheless, what remains is the notion of how dangerously attractive sunlight can be for Danes.

That is why, when spring arrives, Danes wake up from their hygge hibernation – we essentially turn into a nation of cats – seeking out places where they can soak up the sun. But it is not just Danes who covet daylight.

Natural light is often considered a key feature people look for when buying a home. People value natural light within indoor spaces and will pay more for sunlit real estate. One study by the MIT Real Estate Innovation Lab examined the value of daylight in office spaces. Using a sample of 5,145 commercial office spaces in Manhattan and controlling for other factors that influence rental prices, the study found that there is a 5 to 6 per cent financial premium for daylight in office rental prices.

Famously, there are three things that matter in property: location, location, location. It turns out, however, when it comes to the hygge home, it is: lighting, lighting, lighting. Integrating natural light into homes, or arranging our homes to make the most of the light we have, reduces the need for artificial lighting and is therefore good for both the wallet and the planet. So make sure you have a place to read by the window.

The Happiness Research Institute has also studied how light is connected with happiness. We have found that people whose homes score 7 or above on a scale from 0 to 10 in terms of light are 11.7 per cent more likely to report high levels of happiness – for the previous day. Further, people are 10 per cent more likely to be happy with their home if they are satisfied with the amount of natural light in it. Light gives the feeling of more space. Research shows that, if possible, installing a window is a great way to turn a small, cramped room into one that feels more spacious. But daylight may have an even more fundamental role to play in our day-to-day wellbeing and how well we sleep at night.

Circadian rhythm

Nearly 150 years have passed since Edison invented the light bulb. We now have instant light at our fingertips. At the flick of a switch, we can light up a room, brightly and efficiently. This makes it easy to forget that every living organism on this planet responds to the sun. So let's rewind the clock a little bit. To a time before Edison's invention.

In 1729, the French scientist Jean-Jacques d'Ortous de Mairan conducted an experiment with the mimosa plant. He had noticed that the leaves opened in the day and closed at night. To find out whether the plant was responding to sunlight, he stored it in a dark cupboard for several days and was surprised to see that even in darkness the plant maintained its daily rhythm, the leaves opening and closing. Plants could 'sense the sun without ever seeing it', he concluded. This was the first hint of an internal clock.

Almost three hundred years later, the phone rang at Michael Rosbash's home in Massachusetts. It was 5 a.m. 'When the landline rings at that hour, normally it is because someone has died,' he said afterwards. Fortunately, it was the Nobel Committee chair, informing him that he and two of his colleagues – Jeffrey Hall at the University of Maine and Michael Young at Rockefeller University – had been awarded the Nobel Prize in medicine for their decades-long work on the circadian clock. 'Circadian' is Latin for 'about

a day'. These three men had discovered how plants, animals and humans adapt their biological rhythm so that it is synchronized with the Earth's revolutions.

The beauty of circadian rhythm is that it allows an organism to anticipate the rising and setting of the sun, rather than simply reacting to it. This is what d'Ortous de Mairan had got wrong. We don't react to the rising sun, we react to the expectation of a sunrise. I think there is a lot of beauty in the knowledge that all plant and all animal behaviour is determined by our light–dark cycle.

Circadian rhythm is our biological clock, responsible for releasing chemicals and hormones into our bodies throughout the day. This includes melatonin, which is connected to sleep. In short, Gloria Estefan was right: the rhythm is going to get you. A simple way to put it is to say that daylight keeps us awake at the right time of day and makes us sleep better at night. But it also has a direct impact on our mood and wellbeing.

The term 'Seasonal Affective Disorder' (SAD) was first used in the mid-1980s to describe a syndrome characterized by depressions that occur annually at the same time each year. However, already in 1806 French physician Philippe Pinel had noted in his treatise on insanity that some of his psychiatric patients got worse 'when the cold weather of December and January set in'. Today, light therapy is sometimes applied as a treatment for SAD. The recommendation is thirty minutes of artificial light daily with an intensity of 10,000 lux for one or two weeks. We experimented briefly with a light-therapy box at the Happiness Research Institute, but even my most sun-loving colleague used it only once or twice, so now it lights up one of the rooms in the Happiness Museum.

In everyday life, we may spend only a couple of hours outside a day. And it may be tricky to get even that in on a workday. Especially in midwinter in Denmark, where you have on average seven minutes of daylight a day. Weekends may be used to stock up on sunshine – and placing yourself close to windows while working during the week also helps. Recently, Aarhus University Hospital in Denmark looked into the connection between daylight and depression among 3,000 employees in Aarhus. It found that people who are outside in daylight two hours a day have a 40 per cent lower risk of becoming depressed. And it is not just in Denmark where lack of sunlight is linked with depression.

In 2002–3, the World Health Organization conducted a survey to improve knowledge on the impact of housing on the physical wellbeing and mental health of residents. The study covered eight cities across Europe from Vilnius in Lithuania to Ferreira do Alentejo in Portugal.

The survey asked 290 questions of 8,519 inhabitants in 3,373 homes, among them whether people had been 'missing daylight' in the last year and whether they 'turn on a light even on bright days because the natural light is not sufficient'.

The health status of the participants was surveyed with questions such as whether they had fallen into or had symptoms of depression such as self-reported sleep disturbance, lack of interest in activities, low self-esteem or loss of appetite.

The study found that people who report inadequate natural light in their homes are at greater risk of depression. Of the people in the study, 13 per cent were depressed, reporting either doctor-diagnosed depression or three or more of the key symptoms of depression. While controlling for factors linked with depression, the study showed that those with a doctor-diagnosed depression were 40 per cent more likely to live in a home with inadequate light, and people with three or more major symptoms of depression were 60 per cent more likely to report inadequate light compared with participants who reported adequate light.

Rigshospitalet, the main hospital in Copenhagen, recently found that patients with depression who are placed in rooms facing north-west (which, here, means less light) spend on average fifty-nine days in the hospital before being discharged, while patients in the more sun-filled south-east-facing rooms spend on average twenty-nine days. The hospital is now doing experiments with 'dynamic light' – artificial light that the brain interprets as natural sunlight – to further explore the effect of sunlight on patients with depression. And in the senior-care sector in Denmark, more than thirty nursing homes have now implemented dynamic light, with similar positive results. In the future, we are likely to see more artificial light mimic the rhythm of the daylight – and with that, let's turn to ways we can use artificial light to create a calming effect.

OK, Meik, you might say, I get it – daylight is good. Enough with the studies. Tell me how to get more daylight.

Well, first of all, lighten up, and second, there is plenty you can do to allow more daylight into your home. Let's start with the only study on architecture to survive from antiquity to today. *De architectura* is a collection of ten books on architecture written in 30–15 BC by Roman architect Marcus Vitruvius Pollio. Covering everything from town planning, temples and aqueducts to Archimedes' screw and siege weapons (in Chapter 5 we will see how good

relationships with your neighbours impact on wellbeing. Spoiler alert: siege weapons are not the way forward); the books were presented to Caesar Augustus as a guide for building projects.

You might recognize the name Vitruvius from Leonardo da Vinci's drawing, *Vitruvian Man*, in which the ideal proportions of the human body are outlined. (Turns out my freakishly long arms are far from ideal – the good news is that I can reach the cookie jar on the very top shelf. No cookies for you, Vitruvius!)

According to Vitruvius, good buildings must have three qualities – *firmitatis*, *utilitatis* and *venustatis* – stability, functionality and beauty; today, this is known as the Vitruvian Triad. He also looked at how big windows needed to be to sufficiently light a room. As you know, in a long room, the end furthest away from the windows is going to be darker.

In order to have enough light from the windows, Vitruvius recommended that the length of the room be a maximum of four to five times the height of the windows. So if the windows are one metre tall, the length of the room should be at most four or five metres. However, these days, most architects work with varying floor-to-window ratios, and there are a number of other factors we need to be mindful of when we want to add more daylight to our homes.

TIP FOR DESIGNING HAPPINESS

7 things to be mindful of when adding daylight

WASH AND TRIM

Dirt on windows reduces the light coming through. Also, pay attention to the effect greenery outside your home is having on the light levels inside – trim around doors and windows. You may want to consider slimmer window frames to maximize the surface of the glass.

UH, SHINY!

Shiny materials bounce the light further into your room. A mirror or a glass cabinet will make the rays travel further. The right flooring can work as a light-friendly reflector. Wooden, ceramic or stone floors with a polished finish will reflect more than carpets or rugs.

USE THE RIGHT COLOUR PALETTE

If you have seen pictures of Scandinavian minimalism, this shouldn't surprise you: walls are usually painted white. In part this is because shades of white make a space brighter, as it reflects rather than absorbs the natural light entering the room.

HEIGHT CAN CHANGE EVERYTHING

The higher up a window is placed on the building, the lighter it will be inside. Windows placed high will let more light into the room and disperse it evenly, while light coming through a low window will stay close to the window. This is why you often see larger windows at the lowest part of the building and smaller ones higher up.

REMOVE THE BLOCKADE

Will half a wall do it, or a divider? Consider whether you need a floor-to-ceiling wall or whether there could be a space at the top to allow light to travel through.

CONSIDER SKYLIGHTS

Skylights can bring in twice as much light as a conventional window and may bring light into a room where a typical window is not an option. One downside, however, is that they don't provide the same orientation, that is, they don't provide you with a view of the outside world, other than a patch of sky, so they should be used wisely.

GET THE BALANCE RIGHT

Consider how you can balance the needs of daylight and privacy. Big windows are great for letting in plenty of sunlight, but we also have a need for privacy. Adding a high-level window or using plants to shield the inside from the outside are options here.

TIP FOR DESIGNING HAPPINESS

design with daylight

Sunlight is so important to our wellbeing it is worth keeping it in mind when designing and decorating your home. Placing furniture near a window will help you soak up the rays. In a perfect world, you can plan by using the path of the sun. My work desk is by the window, where the rays of the rising sun enter the room, whereas we have dinner in a room where the setting sun enters the house. Basically, follow your cat. If there is a strip of light, this is where you sit. Purring optional.

Using light to calm kids down

—

'I hadn't even considered what the light can do to the kids,' says Heidi, a teacher at Frederiksbjerg school in Aarhus.

Overall, the Polar Bears are a well-functioning class (just to clarify – that is the name of the class – there aren't actually any polar bears in Danish schools: they get all their education in Greenland), but some pupils had trouble concentrating at the end of the day.

Heidi explains, 'There is one boy, for instance, who loses his concentration and starts rolling around on the floor. If we have the overhead light on, the kids think that they can lie anywhere – but when we turn these pendants on, their focus is on the table. They are like moths. They get drawn to the light. To the table. And they know that now it is time to get to work on their homework.' These pendant lights are single light bulbs that give off a warm glow and hang down from the wall or ceiling. In Heidi's experience, these lamps create a focused area, allowing the kids to shut out the distractions around the room. 'The pupils talk with the other kids who are under the same lamp. They create a small community. I was surprised that such a little thing like changing the lamps could have such a large effect.'

The light these pendants emit is warmer and it forms cosy zones of light. It creates an atmosphere of safety and comfort that reminds the kids of home. 'The kids say themselves that the light is more hygge. They spend so much time in school, we should make sure that it is nice for them to be here.'

But it is not only nicer for the kids, it is also nicer for the teachers. As the children make smaller groups around the tables with pendant lighting, the noise in the classroom goes down. The school took part in an experiment run by Imke Wies van Mil. In her industrial Ph.D., in collaboration with Henning Larsen Architects and the Royal Danish Academy of Fine Arts (KADK), she looked at the ways a human-centred design approach grounded in scientific knowledge could create a better learning environment.

One problem Imke Wies van Mil looked at was noise in schools. And she found that by replacing the uniform white sterile light with pendants in four classrooms, the noise was reduced by between one and six decibels in around 75 per cent of the educational settings she measured. A reduction of one decibel is barely noticeable for humans, but three decibels is noticeable and six decibels is very noticeable. A reduction level of six decibels is equivalent to reducing the noise level from that of a conversation in a restaurant to a conversation at home.

What we should learn from the experience of Frederiksbjerg school is of course the importance of light, how it can shape our behaviour and which dials we can turn when we are considering the light design of a room.

You can work with four dials when illuminating a room: spatial pattern, temporal pattern, light spectrum and light level. Spatial pattern is the distribution of light in the field of view. The temporal pattern is how you

present different light at different times of day – maybe bright in the morning and dim at night. Light spectrum is whether you go with a coloured or white light or a warmer or cooler light. Light level is the absolute intensity of light. Are you going with bright or dim or something in between?

When deciding on which light fittings or lamps to choose for a particular room, it is important to keep in mind what function that room has. Think how different a typical office would be to your living room in terms of lighting. An office would generally have a bright, relatively white, uniform and constant type of lighting, while a living room is likely to have warmer, more colourful, more dispersed lighting.

Often we make the mistake of choosing a lamp and not considering the lighting. We fall in love with the appearance of a certain lamp (guilty) and fail to notice how the light shines from the lamp or to consider what function the light needs to fulfil.

When it comes to lighting we also need to keep in mind where we are placing the lamp, which function it should have and which mood we want to set in that room. A nice soft, warm light may be lovely for having dinner or a glass of wine, but when we have to do the dishes later we need a brighter light to see what we are doing.

You are likely to use each room for different things. I might eat dinner, write or sew a button on my blazer at the dinner table, and I need a certain type of light for each of those activities. It is a good idea to mix different lamps and kinds of light to serve specific needs. You may want to have general lighting from the ceiling, with a focused light from a lamp placed where you need it, and a downward, mood-setting light, to be used whenever needed.

Not all rooms are easy to light. A shiny floor or a metal table might reflect the light, low ceilings might make it difficult to hang pendant lamps, or beams may break the flow of light. But there are so many options with lighting, so there is always a way to make a room more hygge, with just the flick of a switch.

TIP FOR DESIGNING HAPPINESS

choose your lighting

Understanding the purpose of the light you are bringing into your home is essential before deciding what sort of style or fittings you choose. Here are the four main categories of lighting and the best ways to achieve them:

DIFFUSED, SPREAD-OUT LIGHT

Use this for the general lighting of the room. Go for ceiling or wall lamps with glass screens or loose fabric.

FOCUSED, CONCENTRATED LIGHT

Use this for your workstation or where you want to bring attention to details such as paintings or photos. Go for spots or small lamps with a tightly covered shade in either metal or fabric.

UPWARD LIGHT

Use this to supplement the
general lighting in the room or
for lighting for effect. Go for
wall lamps or uplights.

DOWNWARD LIGHT

Use this for your reading corner, or
hyggekrog. Go for floor lamps or
lamps with a closed shade.

Hygge: islands of light

Hygge is about an atmosphere, and lighting is an essential tool for achieving this. The not-so-dark secret to having hygge lighting in your room is to have a lot of smaller sources of light with warm, downward-shining light. The key is to create a warm, calm atmosphere with pockets or islands of light. In contrast, a chandelier hanging from the ceiling will make the room seem colder, especially if you have white walls that reflect the light from above.

Remember you can mix floor lamps, table lamps and ceiling lights to cater for the different needs and functions in the room. A ceiling light will seldom give a hygge glow but can be useful when cleaning the room, for example. Choosing your light starts with considering the function of the room and what you need and use it for.

DINNER-TABLE LIGHT – if you have a pendant, it should be about 50–60 centimetres above the table and it should not create a glare in your eyes or obstruct the view across the table. You want to be able to see your dinner guests.

50–60
centimetres

DINING ROOM – consider two pendants if you have a long table; otherwise, I'd suggest wall-mounted lights or floor lamps so that you have a soft upward light rather than a bright overhead one.

BATHROOM – make sure the light by your mirror presents colours in their exact expression. One time I was going to a fancy-dress party and had dressed up as a Smurf – blue face, blue shirt, white pants, shoes and hat: done. The only problem was, it wasn't a fancy-dress party – it was a Halloween party full of vampires, ghosts, witches, werewolves and a not-so-scary Smurf. Anyway, after the party I washed the blue paint off my face in the bathroom, but the light there was deceptive. To cut a long story short, I spent the next day explaining why I was blue in the face.

BEDROOM – as with most rooms, it's important to have a ceiling light for when you need to clean, but otherwise I think two bedside lamps with a warm hue are sufficient to create a calming atmosphere. It's also a good idea if your bedside lamp has an arm or can be moved around so you can read without disturbing your bed buddy.

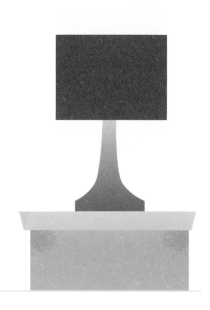

OFFICE – make sure there is not too much contrast between your bright computer screen and the rest of the room, as this can make your eyes tired. Although hygge is always the priority, it's also important to focus when you're at work, so I'd suggest keeping the light level high with some uplighting and a focused light on your desk.

LIVING ROOM – be mindful of dark corners. They can make the room seem smaller but can be taken care of with a fun lamp (this is where you get to use the really jazzy one you couldn't resist from that vintage shop). This is the space to achieve maximum hygge, so I'd suggest that you use mostly downward lighting.

Beyond the home: lighting up the town

—

Rjukan, a small town of 3,000 people, sits at the base of a valley between two mountains in southern Norway. Because of its two towering neighbours, the town is in shadow for half the year. The people in the town can see the sunlight on the mountainside to the north, going up and down but never reaching the town, leaving them in the shade. Consequently, people talk about the sun a lot. 'When is the sun coming back?' they ask. 'When was the last time we saw the sun?'

A Norwegian oil company gifted a cable car to the townspeople, allowing them to get up high on the mountainside during winter to bask in some sunlight. But recently, Martin Andersen, an artist living in the town, came up with an idea. A – shall we say? – 'bright' idea. Mirrors. Giant mirrors.

Each measures 17 square metres, and three are now installed on the mountain above the town in such a way that they turn to track the path of the sun and reflect the sunlight into the heart of the town – the town square. In January, you can find the sunlight there for two hours at least, from midday to 2 p.m. And you'll not only find the sunlight, you'll also find a group of smiling people.

THE ARCHITECTURE OF
HAPPINESS CHECKLIST

———

❑ Daylight is vital to your wellbeing – and natural light should
be seen as a key tool for designing and using happy spaces,
so do everything you can to increase those rays inside.

❑ Consider the four different dials – spatial pattern, temporal
pattern, light spectrum and light level – when deciding how
to brighten your home with artificial light.

❑ Use lighting to influence atmosphere, mood and behaviour.
Warm, soft, downward lighting will add hygge to your home
so use it to your advantage in the right places.

SPACE FOR

HYGGE

The average Danish and British household enjoys 1.9 rooms per person. Canadians enjoy far more space, with 2.6 rooms, and Russians enjoy less, with 0.9 rooms per person. From a European and North American perspective, 1.9 rooms per person is fairly average.

However, with rent going up in places like London and Copenhagen and across the world, it is no longer just students who share flats. The number of people in bigger cities living in a house share or a house with multiple occupation – where more than one household shares a basic amenity such as cooking or bathroom facilities – is increasing. According to Inside Housing, the number of houses in multiple occupation increased by 20 per cent between 2012 and 2020.

I was part of this statistic when I was first setting up the Happiness Research Institute and could not afford to pay rent for my flat by myself. I was well into my thirties and needed two flatmates to make ends meet.

While living with other people has benefits, overcrowded housing can have a negative impact on our wellbeing – and that's on both our physical and our mental health. This became even more evident during the Covid-19 pandemic.

'Every time someone coughs, I get scared,' Silvia, who lives in Croydon, south London, in a shared flat with four people she doesn't know, said during the pandemic. 'I try to stay in my room, but we all share the kitchen and the bathroom.'

One analysis by the New Policy Institute showed that the five most crowded areas in the UK experienced 70 per cent more coronavirus cases than the

five least crowded, even with the data being controlled for the higher infection rate in London. It's easy to see how this happens – crowding undermines our ability to maintain social distance, whereas bigger homes are more likely to have spare bedrooms and more than one bathroom. So when Hollywood celebrities sang 'Imagine' from their mansions to help people get through the pandemic, some people were not amused.

During the pandemic, we conducted a longitudinal study at the Happiness Research Institute. When I say 'longitudinal', I mean that we followed a group of people over time so we could see the change in their wellbeing. We started our research process with a baseline survey on 13 April 2020 and continued to survey the same people over time on a weekly to monthly basis. The analysis was based on six rounds of surveys which in total stretched over three months into the pandemic and consisted of 11,000 observations from more than 4,000 individuals in 97 countries.

We asked how many people the participants were sharing their household with and how big their homes were to get an indication of how crowded their living conditions were. In short, we asked a lot of people a lot of questions over a long period of time.

What we found was that the more crowded the space, the less satisfied people were with life. For instance, 74 per cent of people in homes with over 75 square metres per person said they were satisfied with life; however, this feeling of satisfaction was true of only 67 per cent of people who had less than 75 square metres per person. Interestingly, this was only the case if they were living with other people. People who lived alone reported being less happy the bigger the space they had.

THE IMPACT OF SPACE ON HAPPINESS

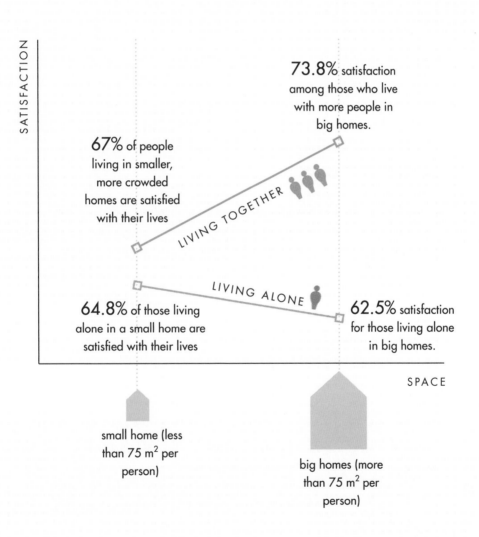

73.8% satisfaction among those who live with more people in big homes.

67% of people living in smaller, more crowded homes are satisfied with their lives

LIVING TOGETHER

LIVING ALONE

64.8% of those living alone in a small home are satisfied with their lives

62.5% satisfaction for those living alone in big homes.

SATISFACTION

SPACE

small home (less than 75 m² per person)

big homes (more than 75 m² per person)

And the importance of space in our homes affects us beyond the time of the pandemic. When we examined the 13,480 homes in the study we did for Kingfisher before the pandemic, we tested the ways in which different issues limited how happy people were with their homes. How did poor natural light or poor air quality or lack of green spaces undermine happiness in the home and with the home?

The basics need to be in place. If the air quality is bad, if the spaces are too dark, or too cold, of course we are not happy with our homes. In fact, these factors can threaten our mental and physical health, which brings us back to the second crucial level on Maslow's pyramid of needs – if they do not feel safe and secure, our homes can prevent us from feeling happy, fulfilled and able to achieve our goals.

Unfortunately, these issues are not uncommon. In the ten countries we focused on, we saw that, for instance, 9 per cent of people reported bad air quality in their homes and 16 per cent were unhappy with the temperature in their building. However, the lack of space was the most common issue: 20 per cent of the people in the study reported that they lacked space in their homes. And this was also the issue that seemed to undermine happiness the most. We found that lack of space is the most important factor explaining why some people are less happy with their homes than others.

Mess causes stress. If our home is very small and therefore cramped and cluttered, most of us will be unhappier with it. Thank you, big data, for that nugget of wisdom, you might say. But here is the kicker. The size is not the key element – the key element is spaciousness.

In our study we tested both size and spaciousness: we asked people to report how large their home was objectively – how many square metres or feet, or how many rooms – but we also asked them whether they felt that their home was spacious. When we analysed the data from the 13,480 homes in the study, we discovered a myth that a lot of us might be carrying around: that we are happier if we live in a larger home.

Yes, we know that if we were to live in a very small and cluttered home, most of us would dislike it, but the size of your home and how many rooms you have matters only up to a certain point. What we found is that it is the subjective feeling of a cramped home that is the problem, not the objective size of the home itself. Most importantly, we found that the perception of space is three times more important than actual size when it comes to being happy with your home.

In other words, the number of square metres or square feet occupied has less to do with why some people are happier with their homes than the perception of space does. Interestingly, the perception of space and actual space is not very correlated. A large home can feel cluttered and small, while a small home can look and feel spacious. That is good news for those of us living in the bigger cities or on smaller budgets.

TIP FOR DESIGNING HAPPINESS

add space, not size

The takeaway here is that our perception of space is strongly related to how we design and furnish our home and whether it is cluttered or not, and so the question becomes not how we get a bigger home but how we can use design to make us feel happier about our home by designing for spaciousness.

CHOOSE FURNITURE ACCORDING TO THE SIZE OF THE ROOM

A huge sofa in a small room is going to make the room look cramped no matter what, so make sure to measure your space and think about sleeker options. Consider modular sofas that come in parts so you can arrange them in a layout that best suits your space. These are also a great option if you would struggle getting a solid sofa up the stairs and into your flat.

CONSIDER HOW ROOMS OR FURNITURE CAN HAVE MULTIPLE FEATURES

When Joey and Chandler get tired of sharing their apartment with Ross in the TV series *Friends*, they try to get him to rent a horrible apartment with a kitchen/bathroom. This is not what I am talking about. It might be that your living room can be turned into a guest room if you have guests coming from out of town, or you might have a work desk that can be folded away when it is not needed. Appreciating the ways in which your space can be multifunctional will give it more value.

ALLOW FOR AS MUCH SUNLIGHT AS POSSIBLE

As I discussed earlier, more light will increase the perception of space. Low-budget solutions are cleaning your windows regularly or adding a mirror; higher-end solutions include adding a skylight. Think about whether to have blinds or curtains around your windows, as long, heavy curtains can take up valuable wall space and feel cumbersome in small spaces, although they can be a nice design feature and keep in the warmth in larger rooms.

USE YOUR SPACE VERTICALLY

Don't be a square – think in cubic metres. Can you place shelves higher up on the wall? Can you elevate your kids' bed and give them a space to play underneath – or how about turning the useless space under the stairs into an awesome Happy Potter tribute playroom? There is no end of inspiration for how to store your stuff in nifty ways on Instagram, and I recommend scrolling through the genius solutions on #storageideas.

CONSIDER INTERNAL SLIDING DOORS

If you are short on space, consider whether some of your doors could glide open along a fixed track instead of opening out or in, which saves the extra space taken up by the arc of a conventional door. Connecting the kitchen and dining room with a sliding door could allow you to have a larger dining table or additional cupboards in the kitchen. But keep in mind that a sliding door is not as soundproof as a regular door, so you might prefer one between your kitchen and living area rather than between your bedroom and living area.

ONE IN, ONE OUT

Go by the principle that if something has to come into your home, something else has to go. Ideally, you will only replace things that are broken and that you loved. That way you will never end up with drawers full of old, broken, meaningless objects and instead fill your drawers with useful items.

Pre-cluttering

—

When I was a kid, we had a cookbook in our house that would fall open to the page with the pancake recipe on it. I've always been a big fan of pancakes. Happiness comes in many shapes – pancake is one of them.

This is why an ad from my local supermarket caught my attention this morning. It was for a batter dispenser and featured a pancake. 'Get the perfect amount every time!' it said. When making pancakes, you fill it with batter and then dispense a scientifically precise amount into the pan.

We all know how bad a pancake tastes if it is a different size compared to the one we just ate. Horrible, right? And we all love cleaning an additional item when we have made pancakes, right? The answer? Get additional stuff to fill up your kitchen! Enjoy having more stuff to clean! Don't use it for ten years, then have to go to the recycling station to throw it out!

I am sure you are familiar with Marie Kondo and her KonMari strategy to declutter you home. If not, you may have a lot of stuff under that rock you have been living under for the past few years but, briefly put, she says that to declutter your home you should place all similar items on the floor – say, your clothes or batter dispensers – then touch them one by one. If the item doesn't 'spark joy', it should be thanked for its service then donated or thrown out.

A more sustainable approach to decluttering and just throwing your stuff away is to host a going-away party. No, you are not going away – your things are. The last time I moved I found a range of things that I had not used for years. So one afternoon I invited a few friends over for coffee and cake and laid out the things that were up for grabs. Needless to say, they all found grateful new homes.

But I think we can and should do much better. Marie Kondo, you know what would spark joy? Buying less crap. Don't bring that batter dispenser into your home in the first place. You know those warning stickers they put on cigarettes? I think we need warning stickers on a lot of stuff. Guaranteed NOT to make you happy. Perhaps Benjamin Franklin said it best: 'The bitterness of poor quality remains long after the sweetness of low price is forgotten.'

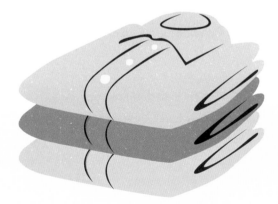

The Diderot Effect: why we want things we don't need

———

In 1769 French philosopher Denis Diderot wrote an essay about an unhappy experience. It all started when he acquired a beautiful scarlet robe. Prior to the purchase, Diderot had been living in poverty, but he had recently sold his collection of books to Catherine the Great, Empress of Russia, for a hefty sum. Shortly thereafter, Diderot acquired the robe, but rather than making him happy, it made him miserable.

The robe was so beautiful and luxurious that he started to notice how it seemed out of place when surrounded by the rest of his common and shabby possessions. You may be familiar with that feeling you get after buying a new shirt and suddenly noticing that your trousers look old and worn out – or you buy a new sofa and then the coffee table starts to look like it needs an upgrade.

'There is no longer any unity,' wrote Diderot in the essay 'Regrets on parting with my old dressing gown'. He then went out and bought more new stuff. A new mirror to put above the mantle, new paintings, a new rug from Damascus, new sculptures, an expensive clock, a new bureau and a leather chair to replace his old chair, which was put in storage. Soon the apartment was completely refurnished, all because of the scarlet robe.

The Diderot Effect means that when you buy a new thing it can create a spiral of consumption that leads you to desire and acquire more new things which your former self didn't need in order to feel happy.

That is why the Hemnes dresser from Ikea goes with the Hemnes sofa bed, the Hemnes bedside table, the Hemnes display cabinet and the Hemnes shoe closet with two drawers. Sets of furniture are always showcased for an entire room. The question is whether we can ignore the Hemnes sofa calling for its friends or whether we yield and have to get every piece of the set. Or in the words of Diderot, 'I was absolute master of my old dressing gown – but I have become a slave to my new one.'

Say you save £1,000 and invest the money in the global stock market. Some years are good. Some years are bad. But historically, the average annual return is 7 per cent and, because of the magic of compound interest, this means it will double every ten years. In thirty years, your £1,000 will turn in to £8,000.

Often we buy something because of a fantasy attached to it. We may desire to be a happy family baking pancakes with the kids, so we buy a dough dispenser, instead of simply making pancakes. Will I be more likely to bake pancakes with this dough dispenser or will I be more likely to spend time looking for things in my cluttered kitchen cabinets?

Get recognition from people because of the life you live, not because of the things you have. Remember, it is better to have stories to tell than stuff to show.

TIP FOR DESIGNING HAPPINESS

---

pre-clutter

When we are aware of the mechanism, we can start to register and observe it when it kicks in and start to question or even fight it. Here are some tips for pre-cluttering.

PRETEND THAT YOU ARE MOVING

The average Dane moves six times during their lifetime. I am up to ten times already. So when considering whether to buy an item, think about whether you would like to wrap it up, put it in a box, carry it to the removal van then take it out of the van and into your new place. Six times. For me, the answer would be certainly, for the mementos that mean a lot to me. For a batter dispenser, not so much.

THINK OF THE MONEY YOUR MONEY COULD MAKE YOU

If you don't buy stuff, you will have more money to put to work for you, so you have to work less, so you have time for what actually makes you happy (making pancakes with your family – not having a batter dispenser).

THINK OF THE COST IN TERMS OF TIME

On Amazon there is a dog's throwing toy shaped like a football for $41. The blurb says that this toy strengthens your dog's mind and stops it nibbling your belongings. In addition, it bounces really well and you can use it to throw in the park and the yard. I know, right, the park and the yard. Wait, you know what you could also throw in the park and the yard? A stick.

Well, you might say, it's only $41 and my wallet is becoming too tight for my fifties. However, odds are that you have to work more to get more money. When I was working as a baker, taking shifts between midnight and the morning, I would earn around 120 kroner per hour, or around $20. So it would take me about two hours to earn $41. However, taxes in Denmark are around 50 per cent, so I would actually have to work around four hours to make enough money to buy the toy. Or perhaps 4.5 hours if I add in the time it took me to ride my bike to the bakery at midnight. Or I could just play with my dog for 4.5 hours. What do you think would make it happier? Oh, look, there's a stick!

In the words of Henry David Thoreau, 'The cost of a thing is the amount of what I will call life which is required to be exchanged for it, immediately or in the long run.'

If you still want to buy the $41 toy shaped like a football, go for it, but thinking this way can help you distinguish between things you truly value and meaningless stuff you and your dog don't really need.

Be mindful of hygge washing

—

One of my favourite TV shows is *Mad Men*. If you don't know it, it is set in the advertising industry in the sixties. The main character, Don Draper, declares, 'Advertising is about one thing: happiness' – so I can almost put it down as research and watch it with good conscience.

In the episode 'The Gold Violin', the head of the ad agency, Bertram Cooper, points out the foundation of the advertising business. 'People buy things to realize their aspirations,' he says, pointing to a Rothko painting he has just purchased. And indeed, there have been many adverts that rely on happiness as the main creative concept. The concept of happiness in adverts is in fact so common that in 2016 Coca-Cola decided to drop their 'Open Happiness' slogan from 2009 because 'happiness is overused'.

The greatest threat to capitalism is everyone feeling happy enough that they no longer need to buy anything to make them so. Which means that staying at home and finding comfort and joy in what you already have is an act of rebellion. This is what hygge is truly all about – living the good life on a tight budget. It is the enjoyment of simple pleasures. It is the art of creating a nice, warm, comforting atmosphere.

I think one of the best things we can give to our children is an understanding of where we can find joy and wellbeing without spending money. And one of my main areas of focus at the Happiness Research Institute has to do with exploring how we can decouple wealth from wellbeing and most efficiently convert wealth into wellbeing. I believe hygge can be a vital ingredient in this endeavour, as it does not require a full wallet. It is not extravagant and wasteful. Hygge is about making the best of what we have.

However, when hygge went beyond Denmark, a few things got lost in translation. This first occurred to me when an American journalist asked me, 'If I want to get hygge, what's the first thing I should buy?'

As hygge grew in popularity, companies tried to market their products to fit the trend. Even when it seems like they are stretching the concept a little too far, like putting the word 'hygge' on things such as subscription boxes and detox soups – things that Danes wouldn't associate with hygge.

As Charlotte Higgins pointed out in the *Guardian*, 'I have seen hygge used to sell cashmere cardigans, wine, wallpaper, vegan shepherd's pie, sewing patterns, a skincare range, teeny-tiny festive harnesses for dachshunds, yoga retreats and a holiday in a "shepherd's hut" in Kent.' I think hygge has been hijacked by corporate players the same way yoga and mindfulness were. If something becomes popular, companies are going to try to make money out of it and crash that party.

When yoga became popular, companies started selling $100 yoga pants. And to take your mindfulness to the next level, you could buy a mindfulness plate to eat off. They cost only $19.95. Do you feel present now? So I was happy to read a piece in *The New York Times* in which futurist Lucie Greene called hygge a reaction to the earlier 'wellbeing movement', which seemed to focus on '$100 Lululemon leggings and $10 bottles of cold-pressed juices'. Because, at its heart, hygge is not about expensive things, it is more about an atmosphere, a certain sensation or feeling, and this comes for free in simple, humble forms. Sometimes, less is more hygge.

Not only did we shake our heads over the misinterpretation of hygge, we formed a council – a hygge council with the aim of ensuring that hygge was put on UNESCO's Intangible Cultural Heritage list. Spain has flamenco, Italy has pizza baking, Belgium has beer culture – Denmark has nothing on the list. So the hygge council tried to get hygge on the list to protect and preserve the original meaning of the word. Full disclosure: I am on the council. And yes, we did have pastries for our meetings there. Our first bid failed – but the fight goes on.

So when you see anything being sold as 'hygge', stop and think whether that item is really going to change the atmosphere of your home or bring joy to your life. If it will, great! But hygge is not about having it all. It is about enjoying what you have and enjoying it with the people in your life. It is not about what you have but the atmosphere you create. It's a state of mind. It's what makes a place feel like home.

In that sense, hygge is about being frugal – about old virtues. It is about following the tradition of earlier generations, the generations that didn't throw away things because they were broken but learned how to fix them. It is about repairing our clothes rather than buying new ones. It is about using the food that we have in our fridge and not letting it go to waste.

The importance of green spaces

—

Now that so many of us are living in cities, having an outdoor space to call our own is a real luxury, and if we do have one it can be the most coveted part of our property. Barbecues and picnics in the garden while soaking up the fresh air can be a great way to have a hygge time with your friends and family, but it isn't essential. I've lived the majority of my life in places that didn't have a garden, but I have always found that adding a lot of plants adds to the hygge. Bringing plants into different rooms is a way to connect the indoors with the outdoors – and it turns out green is not only good for hygge but also good for our health.

What is now considered a landmark study, published in 1984 in *Science* by environmental psychologist Roger Ulrich, demonstrated the healing power of plants. Ulrich and his team were some of the first to use the standards of modern medical research such as experimental controls and quantified health outcomes to examine whether having a view of a garden can speed healing from surgery. Remember this was 1984, when songs such as 'Karma Chameleon' were in the music charts – so both science and music were still developing.

The team of researchers reviewed the medical records of people recovering from gallbladder surgery in a hospital in Pennsylvania. Some patients had a view of trees, some had a view of a brick wall. Controlling for all other factors, the researchers found that patients who could look at the green trees healed on average one day faster, had fewer post-surgical complications and needed significantly less pain medicine than their wall-facing counterparts. So not only daylight but also nature will hopefully find their way to the toolbox when we plan and design hospitals in the future.

'Gee, that's great, Doc,' you might say, 'so I should have a view of a park and not the building opposite me. I wish I could afford that!'

The good news here is that Ulrich followed up with another study in 1993, this time at Uppsala University Hospital in Sweden. This time, 160 patients who had undergone heart surgery and were in the intensive care unit were randomly assigned one of six views. A large photograph of a tree-lined stream, a large photograph of a shadowy forest, a blank wall, a white panel, or one of two different abstract paintings.

The study found that the patients with the large photograph of the stream and trees were less anxious and needed fewer doses of strong pain medicine than those with the darker forest photograph, the abstract art or the blank wall or white panel.

Let's be clear about one thing. Looking at a picture of a tree-lined stream is not going to cure cancer. But there are convincing studies that show that looking at scenes of greenery and nature can reduce pain and stress, and since stress has a negative effect on your immune system, there are health and wellbeing benefits to be harvested from garden gazing (pun intended).

A less scientific way of getting to the same conclusion is by logging on to Instagram and recognizing that there are more than 3.2 million posts with the hashtag plantsmakepeoplehappy. There are many reasons why having plants in our homes makes us happy. There is research that shows that a large number of plants can purify the air we breathe, particularly Spider Plants, Boston Ferns and Ficus Trees. Caring for plants is also shown to reduce stress and boost your mood because it allows you to focus on something natural away from a screen, and also experience the rewards of caring for something that you can watch flourish. So, whether you post about them on your Instagram or not, your houseplants are doing much more for you than just making your home look nice and green.

While houseplants are a no-brainer for creating more hygge at home, remember that our gardens should be filled with a variety of plants too. A big, open lawn is boring to look at and not very hygge. We need to apply the same rules to our outdoor space as we do to our indoor space.

TIP FOR DESIGNING HAPPINESS

how to make the most of your green space

You need different spaces to create the hygge. That goes for outside as well as inside. Ideally, you want different spaces for different activities. And one of the activities is of course to have a hygge time in the hygge space in your garden.

It's the same with towns and streets. If you can see a mile ahead what is coming, it is less interesting to walk around than it would be in the crooked streets you find in European town centres from medieval times. The curvy streets hold promises of a new discovery around every corner. The same goes for gardens. If you can create small spaces, it will be more interesting to walk around – and it will be more hygge. You want to aim to create small, cosy spaces where you can get your hygge on. There are plenty of options, depending on the size of your budget and your garden, from building walls and planting trees or hedges to more temporary options like trellises and pergolas.

If you have a terrace with a table and some chairs, you can hyggefy the space by surrounding the table and chairs with some pots with plants in them to give the sensation of a protected space. This can also be a way to create the right microclimate for your hygge space. You want to make a place where you would be happy to spend a few hours with a book on your lap and your feet on the table.

Beyond the home: adding green space to urban environments

Cities throughout the world, but especially in North America, are struggling with rampant urban sprawl or suburban sprawl – a rapid expansion of the geographic extent of cities and towns – often characterized by low population density and increased reliance on cars for transportation and with little concern for urban design or planning. The negative consequences of this phenomenon include higher air pollution and increased traffic congestion and traffic fatalities.

These negative consequences are the reason why the Copenhagen Five Finger plan enjoys iconic status as a model for urban development and has been guiding the development for greater Copenhagen for more than a generation. The first Finger Plan was designed in 1947.

The old part of Copenhagen was considered to be the palm of a hand and had yet to be developed as the natural centre of the city, but the plan was that Copenhagen was to grow outwards in five fingers linked to the railway system and road networks. But between the five fingers were green wedges exempt from urban development, to keep the woods and recreational areas. The idea was to ensure that the citizens of the new suburbs along the fingers would have the shortest possible distance to a green and open landscape. Nature at the front door. Space between the cities.

This isn't the case in every city, but another example is London, where public green space covers 16.8 per cent of the city and is home to 8 million trees. The capital was recently awarded the status of being the world's first National Park City (NPC) under a new initiative to help improve life in cities by working with residents, visitors and partners and encouraging people to enjoy the outdoors more and to make the city greener, healthier and wilder. Launched by the National Park City Foundation (NPCF), in partnership with World Urban Parks and Salzburg Global Seminar, the initiative aims to name at least twenty-five National Park Cities by 2025 and is already in discussion with other UK and world cities to help them gain NPC status. While not every city is as lucky, this initiative is just one of many trying to make sure that green space is available for all – so watch this space.

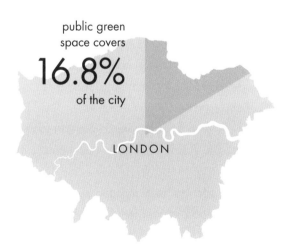

public green
space covers
16.8%
of the city

LONDON

Hygge: the good life on a tight budget

—

I think my favourite hike in the world is around Hammerknuden in the area around Hammershus – the house of the hammer – on Bornholm. Hammershus was completed in the late thirteenth century and was Scandinavia's largest medieval fortification. It rests on a hilltop overlooking the Baltic Sea and is surrounded by lush forest and rocky hills, and is particularly impressive when the heather blooms in late summer. At the foot of the steep cliff you can see lion and camel heads – animal-shaped rocks rising out of the sea – and Hammer, Opal and Krystal lakes nearby, their names like something from *The Lord of the Rings*.

Juniper for your gin and tonic grows in several places, and rosehips for your jams or chutneys by the coast – and chanterelle mushrooms in a secret location I will never tell. Goats are having siestas on the rocks overlooking the lakes while sheep graze on the walking trails. They usually get out of your way – you will only have to swerve when a Scottish long-horn cow is coming in the opposite direction. This is as close to rush hour as it gets on Bornholm.

With scenery like this and the fresh sea air in your lungs, it should come as no surprise that placing one foot in front of the other brings a range of

impressive benefits, both physical and mental, and so one of my favourite activities will always be hiking, whether it's longer stretches on Bornholm with my trusted backpack and Thermos or my daily evening walk around the green space in the city. When I move to a new neighborhood in Copenhagen, the first thing I do is explore which streets and areas provide the most trees and green spaces and create my daily walking tour around those. No matter where you live, there will be somewhere nearby that you can do the same.

Living a hygge life and making a hygge home means understanding that happiness does not have to come with a price tag. It means learning how we can separate what we have from how we feel. Hygge can be felt anywhere, by anyone, so take notice when activities bring you joy and are free, or inexpensive. Hygge is about living the good life on a low budget and using your space for living rather than for storage of your stuff. Hygge is what turns your house into a home.

THE ARCHITECTURE OF
HAPPINESS CHECKLIST

❑ Can you make your space more spacious? Find new homes for the stuff you no longer love and use pre-cluttering to add space to your place. Not buying stuff you don't need in the first place is what sparks real joy.

❑ Be mindful of the Diderot Effect and hygge washing. Don't let companies define what hygge is; remember, it is first and foremost about connection and atmosphere – not things.

❑ Green is good. Green works. Whether people are in a hospital, at home or simply walking along a tree-lined street, plants have been proven again and again to have a positive effect on our wellbeing, so bring them into your home too.

HOW TO
DESIGN FOR
CONNECTION

A hygge home is a place that offers connection. A sense of togetherness. Somewhere you feel surrounded by people who know you well and have your back. A hygge home is a social home or, to put it in the words of the great Ralph Waldo Emerson, 'The ornament of a house is the friends who frequent it.'

Every year, I make the same New Year's resolution. I want to have friends over for dinner once a month in the coming year. I always fail in the mission – travel, deadlines and coronaviruses get in the way – but the ambition does mean that I have more people over than if I had not stated it.

One of the most consistent results from the research on happiness is the importance of our relationships with other people. They are what give purpose and meaning to our lives, and one of the most important ingredients in the recipe for happiness. It is no surprise that the need for social connection and belonging are central in Maslow's pyramid. And the greatest sense of belonging – the most hygge moments – I have experienced has seldom been in Michelin-starred restaurants – it's been in the homes of family and friends, eating good food in great company.

If I could pass a universal law, I would give everybody one additional good friend – and make sure that nobody feels left out. And I believe the way we design our homes and neighbourhoods can play an important part in that ambition. We need to consider both how we get people to meet in the first place and how we get people to connect, then make sure that no one feels left out and that we form meaningful relationships.

Happiness for dinner

—

My favourite table is the dinner table. The dinner table is a unifier, a place of community. It is where we connect. It is where we learn about the world, where our language is developed and where we reconnect with our loved ones. For the past decade, I've been interested in the question, how can we eat better? Not just from a nutritional perspective, but from a happiness one as well.

The good news is that there is a lot of evidence of the wellbeing value of family dinners. A range of different studies has shown that family meals are associated with higher average grades for teenagers, a stronger sense of belonging, better communication skills, less obesity and fewer depressive symptoms, even after the study was controlled for family connectedness.

The bad news is that in certain countries family dinners have been on the decline. Fifty-nine per cent of Americans report that their family today have fewer family dinners than when they were growing up. The majority of American families report eating a single meal together fewer than five days a week, and the average American eats one in every five meals in the car, according to the *Atlantic*. These numbers were reported in 2014, and I fear they have not improved since then.

And things aren't looking any better in the UK. One survey by the Social Issues Research Centre in 2018 found that the average British dinner lasts just twenty-one minutes and is often eaten in front of the TV. Dining tables have been relegated for use only on special occasions and the research reveals that a fifth of British households no longer even own one. I am no stranger to the joy of eating in front of the telly. In my house it is almost a tradition on 1 January. But it is more the exception than the rule.

The table is where I connect with my loved ones. This is where I hear about their day. Where we talk about highs and lows, the past, the present and the future and, most importantly, where I practise my dad-joke material. (What did the lobster say to the lobster that was eating all the mussels? Don't be so shellfish.) In short, it is the best part of my day.

Eating in front of the TV is fine from time to time, but if we never have dinner at the table, we lose out on an investment that yields a high happiness return. The dinner table is the one place where you can have a positive impact on the physical and mental wellbeing of your friends and family. And I am not alone in hoping for more family dinners. The study from the Social Issues Research Centre also showed that 47 per cent of Brits said that they would like to have more family dinners, either at home or at a family member's house, and 49 per cent of people in Britain consider family dinners to be the most important way of spending quality time together.

TIP FOR DESIGNING HAPPINESS

consider which meals give you longer family dinners

One way to have more table time with your friends and family is to serve them food which they have to work for. The more of the cooking process you can move to the table, the better. The dishes below make great non-TV dinners.

DINOSAUR CLAWS

When we eat artichokes at home, the meal usually lasts about twelve minutes longer than when we eat something else. (I've timed it!) Serve them as a side dish or as an appetizer. Prepping time is basically a minute, so it is great in terms of eating time compared to prepping time.

Fill a large pot with salted water and bring to the boil. Halve a lemon and add it to the water, then add the artichokes and cook for about thirty minutes. When the leaves slip off easily, they are done.

Drain the water then serve the artichokes whole with some salted butter. Dip the leaves in butter and harvest the flesh with your teeth and tongue. After you have eaten all the leaves, you will get to a fuzzy field of little inedible hairs. Remove them, and you get to the treasure – the meaty artichoke heart.

And if you want your young kids to get excited about artichokes, just tell them you are making 'dinosaur claws' for dinner.

IT'S A WRAP

As mentioned above, the more of the cooking you can move to the table, the better – in this case, it's more of the assembling. Fresh Vietnamese spring rolls and Mexican tacos are great ways of eating a lot of vegetables and getting your friends or family to take part in the work.

For the spring rolls, chop up carrots, spring onions, some romaine lettuce and cucumber – preferably into slim sticks – and place them on a large dish. Set out peanuts, beansprouts, sliced chilli, mint and coriander, some hoisin sauce and, if you like, some prawns. Place everything in the centre of the table.

Fill a second large dish with hot water and bring it and some sheets of rice paper to the table too. Gather the family to assemble their spring rolls by softening a rice sheet in the hot water, laying their preferred ingredients in a line along the centre and then rolling up the sheet.

If you are in the mood for Mexican food, the principle is the same: place the tortilla wraps and ingredients in the middle of the table and let people assemble the dish themselves. Go for guacamole, onion, black beans, pineapple, coriander and chilli.

SWEET DREAMS ARE MADE OF CHEESE

Who am I to diss a Brie? Yes, it is time to put on Eurythmics and go old school with the eighties answer to tapas. Fondue is, well, fun to do, and it is a sure way to slow down dinner and bring the cooking to the table.

Rub the inside of a cheese fondue pot with a garlic clove, then add one cup of white wine and grate about 500 grammes of cheese (for example a mix of Gruyère and Emmental) and add that to the pot. Cook over a moderate heat and stir until creamy and smooth.

Traditionally, bread cubes are then dipped into the cheese mixture, but I would recommend a selection of your favourite vegetables, either sliced or cubed – try radishes, carrots, peppers or perhaps small roasted potatoes.

By the way, did you hear about the explosion at the cheese factory? The only thing left was debris. (Just in case your teenage kids have friends over for dinner and you don't have anything embarrassing to say.)

The vacant chair principle

——

If you are like me, you may find attending receptions by yourself awkward. One challenge is balancing your canapé and glass of wine while shaking hands, but even before getting to that point there is the 'I don't know anybody here and everybody else is chatting to someone so I'll just check my phone' phase. But I'd like to share a little design hack that can make it easier for you to join in with the conversation.

A few years ago, we at the Happiness Research Institute looked into how different leisure activities were impacting on the wellbeing of young people. One of the initiatives we studied was live-action role-playing games where the participants would act out roles, dress in costumes and use props, for example as orcs and elves in the woods fighting with swords and magic spells. This activity appealed especially to youngsters who would usually be considered introverts and sometimes struggled with traditional sports activities. So, essentially, me thirty years ago.

We followed the participants over time, before they started the activities and, finally, eighteen months after they had begun, and asked them the same questions. By doing this we were able to control for other developments during the period, for example, if their parents had divorced, and work out the effect the activities were having.

What we found was a significant increase in social connectivity among the participants in the role-playing games. Sixteen per cent more of the youngsters now reported being satisfied with their social relationships, and 20 per cent more said they felt they had someone to call on in times of need. Even the level of satisfaction with life – a notoriously difficult needle to move – went up by 12 per cent.

THE POSITIVE IMPACT OF LIVE-ACTION ROLE-PLAY

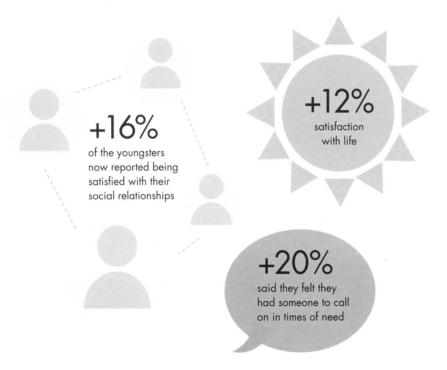

+16%
of the youngsters now reported being satisfied with their social relationships

+12%
satisfaction with life

+20%
said they felt they had someone to call on in times of need

We discovered that not only were the role-playing games really effective in allowing the participants to develop themselves socially, by trying out different roles and identities, enhancing their social skills and empathy and giving them a fun way to exercise while playing the games (usually by running away from hordes of orcs with axes), but also the way they conducted their meetings was noteworthy. Now and then the participants would meet up to plan new events. It was in these meetings that I found out about the vacant chair principle.

The idea was that there should always be a seat free at the table, making it easier for a newcomer to join the group. It was the responsibility of the people already at the table to make sure there was an extra chair for anyone who wanted to join them. This is just one example of a way to design spaces for inclusivity. Similarly, when standing and talking in groups of three or four people, they were asked not to form a full circle but always to leave the circle open for a newcomer to step into and join the conversation.

How we design the social infrastructure and social rules of a space must not be overlooked when we try to create spaces where people thrive. What these orcs and elves managed to do was to create a place where the barriers for entering social interactions were reduced, making it easier for the introverted kids to enter the group. This is such a simple lesson, and one that we can all easily apply in any social situation or at work.

Since seeing the vacant chair principle in action, I have been more mindful of the ways the seating plan impacts on the behaviour and atmosphere in the room. For example, when we are recruiting at the Happiness Research Institute and more than one person is interviewing the candidate, we don't all sit on the opposite side of the table to the candidate. I believe it creates a

more relaxed atmosphere this way, and we want the candidate to be relaxed so that they can show themselves to their best advantage. We want them to understand that we are on the same side.

The shape of hygge

——

Twenty years ago, I had dinner with a group of friends in a restaurant in central Copenhagen. The food was great, the wine was plentiful and the laughter was heartfelt. As we left, the waitress mentioned that it seemed like we had had a good evening.

'You know, we really did. It was exceptional,' I replied.

'It's the magical round table.' She nodded towards it. 'People always have a good time at this table. It's a shame it's the only round table we have.'

That was the first time I became aware of the advantages of sitting at a round table. Of course, the legends of King Arthur should have brought my attention to it sooner. As you probably know, King Arthur would assemble the greatest knights in his kingdom at Camelot, his castle, and gather them at a round table. With a round table, nobody sits at the head of the table and so everyone is positioned as an equal. The round table can therefore be seen as bringing equality and peace, but it also has more everyday advantages – a cosier atmosphere and more space.

A round table allows everybody around it to make eye contact with everybody else, which makes the atmosphere more personal and intimate.

It also means that everyone can take part in the conversation, and it can then become deeper and more personal. Nobody is in charge at the head of the table, and nobody is isolated at the end of it. Also, even if the number of guests is uneven, there is no sense of there being an unfilled place at the table.

In addition, a round table takes up less space than a rectangular one, as the curved edge optimizes the surface area. In order not to play 'eating on the aeroplane', with elbows bumping into each other, a rule of thumb is to give each person sixty centimetres of space so that they can sit comfortably (this does of course also depend on the chairs). A table with a diameter of 150 centimetres gives 471 centimetres of circumference, enough space for eight people. A table 120 centimetres in diameter seats five people.

However, things can get out of hand. The biggest round table I've seen has a circumference of 18 metres. It is called 'The Parliament of Nature' and was designed and crafted for the UN Climate Summit in Copenhagen in 2009. Of course, there is a limit to how large a round table can be; too big, and you would sit further and further away from the people across from you and the conversation would turn into a shouting contest. 'I SAID – THE FISH IS REALLY DELICIOUS!!'

TIP FOR DESIGNING HAPPINESS

---

consider how the chair and table settings
facilitate connection

This means applying the vacant chair principle, but it also means that when you have guests you help them make connections with each other, for example by mentioning some common ground or interest, for example, 'You are probably the two people I know who know most about fermenting.' With a larger group of people, it's helpful to think about the seating plan, and when you're just eating with your family, it's sometimes an idea to mix things up by switching away from the familiar seats at the dinner table to avoid things feeling repetitive.

A hygge conversation

———

Do you feel close to people? Do you feel that there is someone you can turn to? Do you feel there is someone who really knows you well? The answers to these questions are very likely to be connected to your happiness level and your sense of meaning in your life.

In one study published in *Psychological Science* by researchers at the University of Arizona and Washington University in St Louis, the correlation between the types of conversations people have and their levels of happiness was examined. The seventy-nine participants wore an electronic recorder for four days and every twelve and a half minutes a thirty-second clip of the participants' environment was recorded. Each of the 23,689 waking recordings was then analysed to hear whether the participant was alone or engaged in conversation, either in small talk, for example, 'What do you have there? Popcorn? Yummy!' or in a more substantial and meaningful conversation such as 'She fell in love with your dad? So, did they get divorced soon after?'

To estimate happiness levels, the participants were asked questions around wellbeing, such as how satisfied they were with life on a scale from zero to ten, and true-or-false questions such as 'I see myself as someone who is happy, satisfied with life.' The questions were asked twice, three weeks

apart. The results showed that higher levels of wellbeing were associated with spending more time talking to others and further associated with having more meaningful conversations and less small talk.

If we compare the happiest to the least happy participants, the happiest spent 25 per cent less time alone and had twice as many meaningful conversations. Of course, the correlations could also be the other way around: happy people might attract more people or invite deeper conversations. Nevertheless, I believe it works both ways.

The next question is, of course, how do we create more meaningful conversations with people? These days, a lot of people are turning to apps, games or packs of cards designed to spark meaningful conversation. One such game is the hygge game, which promises to create the right atmosphere for a hygge evening 'with more than 300 thought-provoking questions. Cosy conversation in pleasant company. Perfect for a night in, a small party, or a dinner with friends or family.' To be honest, at first, I chuckled at the idea of the hygge game. It seemed too orchestrated. But one Friday in December 2019, as my team at the Happiness Research Institute and I were heading for an after-work glass of gløgg, I brought the game with me.

Questions included: What is your happiest memory of time spent with one or more of your best friends? Did you ever hide anything from your parents when you were a kid? If you could play the main character of any movie, what movie would it be?

These questions sparked hours of fun conversation and the team has since insisted that we bring the game to team dinners and outings. It is a great way to get to know people better and to learn things about them that we would not otherwise know.

US congresswoman Alexandria Ocasio-Cortez mentioned on Instagram that her weekly staff meetings also start with a deck of conversation-starter cards. 'I usually say too much,' she wrote in a post about a conversation card that had read, 'Tell me about a time when your life felt abundant.' According to her, the questions help her team understand each other and bond 'on a more meaningful, human level for a few minutes a week'.

And it is not just Ocasio-Cortez and my team who have enjoyed games like these. One version called Table Topics has sold more than 3.5 million copies. Among the questions are: What topic do you know more about than anyone else in the room? Which era would you visit in a time machine? Have you ever been escorted out of a venue by security?' My answers would be happiness, the fifteenth century and define 'escorted out'.

I think the popularity of these apps and games indicates the demand for something other than stale conversations, and perhaps in today's polarized world conversational competence may be the most overlooked skill. A real conversation – the art of conversation – is a balancing act between talking and listening. This underlines the fact that when we design for connection it is not just about considering the shape of the table but also what we bring to the table in terms of friendly shoulders and open hearts.

TIP FOR DESIGNING HAPPINESS

allow imperfections to be shared

One of the best ways to enable connections to happen is to allow ourselves to be seen, to have the courage to open up and be vulnerable.

The best conversations I've had in my life – conversations that created or forged connections – have frequently begun with me or someone else opening up about struggles or shortcomings. It is interesting that laying out imperfections and vulnerability has most often – although not always – been repaid in kind. Or, to paraphrase one of the greatest philosophers of the twentieth century, Winnie the Pooh, 'You can't stay in your corner of the living room waiting for others to come to you. You have to go to them sometimes.'

Playing with silence

———

Two Danes went fishing. On the first day, they fished and said nothing. On the second day, they fished and said nothing. On the third day, as they were fishing, one of them said, 'Nice weather today,' and the other replied, 'Are we here to fish or to talk?' As I mentioned earlier, Danes are often labelled introverts – and so are my fellow Nordic brothers and sisters.

This might be the case, but perhaps there is also something else at play. The characteristics of Nordic conversation differ from those of other Europeans, or, say, North Americans. We may be more comfortable with silence. There is less of a rapid-fire, fast-paced approach in a Nordic conversation. It is based more on taking turns than what you might call real-time multiplayer style. More chess, less *World of Warcraft*. Or more bowling, less squash. I'm not sure I have the right metaphor here, so bear with me for a second.

If you pause for a moment, it doesn't necessarily mean that it's my turn to speak now; it might just mean that you are thinking about what you are going to say next, collecting your thoughts on the subject you were speaking about. So let's consider redesigning the sound of silence. Why do we think of silence as being awkward? What if the silence need not be awkward but instead reflective, digestive, valuable or comfortable?

———

A good reply is better than a fast reply. A well-thought-out reflection on something I said a week ago means you really listened to what I was saying, perhaps along the lines of 'I've thought a lot about what you said last time about such and such, and perhaps one solution might be . . . ' This can have so much more value than a quick response.

Personally, I've noticed that I speak more slowly when I speak English than when I speak Danish. I need a split-second longer to find the right word and I need to concentrate more. This means I sometimes get a grumpy look on my face – which is kind of an issue when you are a happiness researcher.

One way to learn to become more comfortable with silence is to engage in an activity where the conversation is not the key objective, for example, playing cards, preparing food or solving a puzzle. Also, I find that working with our hands allows us to deal with silence without panicking so much.

The wisest words I've ever heard have often come when people have been holding something in their hands – a tool of some kind, a fishing rod, a pool cue, a paintbrush, a chopping knife, a hand of playing cards, puzzle pieces or a tennis racket. A hygge home puts something in your hands and makes that activity occur naturally and frequently – and this means your words can flow more freely.

The hygge of the commons

———

When I was a kid my brother and I would race on skateboards with the other kids on the street. My brother would always come first, I would always come second and Carsten and Philip, who lived at the top of the street, would always come third and fourth. We lived on a cul-de-sac, so there wasn't much traffic. One of the key selling points for houses in cul-de-sacs is that these dead-end streets reduce the number of cars, and speeding.

I knew nothing about selling points at that age, but I did know the names of all our neighbours and the name of their dogs – one boxer, one golden retriever and one old English sheep dog. My parents were friends with the Perch-Møllers – the family to our right – and we shared a lawnmower. They had the boxer, which was called Sisse. I would play with her and borrow their comic books – the gold standard of neighbours when you are ten.

The epitome of the American dream circa 1960 was the cul-de-sac, and today they remain the cliché of blissful suburban life. Think Wisteria Lane in *Desperate Housewives* – but without the murders. And cul-de-sacs aren't just part of the American dream, they can also increase the price of real estate. Experts in the housing market estimate that potential buyers are willing to pay up to 20 per cent more for a home if it is situated on a cul-de-sac.

By the 1930s, in the US the Federal Housing Authority had embraced the trend of cul-de-sacs; standard street grids had come to be seen as boring and dangerous. In the UK, garden cities such as Welwyn Garden City, founded in 1920, all included cul-de sacs. So, for more than a century, cul-de-sacs have been a tool in how we have designed suburbia. However, for several decades, Wisteria Lane has been falling out of favour. Walk into a city planning meeting with an 'I ♥ cul-de-sacs' T-shirt on and you are likely to be found one week later in a block of concrete. Some of the criticisms are: 'Cul-de-sacs force people to drive more often and longer distances'; 'Cul-de-sacs carve up communities and make them unwalkable'; 'Cul-de-sacs make you fat.'

It's true that people who live in more scattered communities – like suburban cul-de-sacs – drive about 18 per cent more than people who live in dense communities, and studies show that people in dense cities are thinner and have healthier hearts than people who live in spread-out suburbia.

One study by Norman Garrick and Wesley Marshall, assistant professors of engineering at the universities of Connecticut and Colorado respectively, looked at three fundamental metrics of street networks – density, connectivity and configuration – in twenty-four cities in California and how these affected health. They found that areas with more compact street networks have lower levels of obesity, diabetes, high blood pressure and heart disease.

However, according to Thomas Hochschild, Associate Professor of Sociology at Valdosta State University, there might be a very convincing argument for cul-de-sacs: better neighbours. In one study, Hochschild visited 110 homes in Connecticut, a third located on through streets, a third on bulb cul-de-sacs (where houses are splayed out around a circle like the petals of a flower) and a third on dead-end cul-de-sacs, and asked each household about the nature of their relationship with their neighbours. How often do you socialize? Do you help each other out, borrow food from each other . . . ? And so on. There were 150 questions in total.

The homes were in demographically comparable communities and the results were controlled for differences in how long the families had lived there, income, number of children, and so on. What Hochschild found was that the design of the cul-de-sac seemed to facilitate neighbourliness and friendship.

In cul-de-sacs, 40 per cent of people had borrowed or lent food or tools to their neighbours at least once in the previous month. (Yes – I do measure friendships in metrics of how much food you are willing to share.) On the through streets, the figure was 19 per cent.

Around 30 per cent of the people in the cul-de-sacs strongly agreed with the statement 'The friendships and associations I have with my immediate neighbours mean a lot to me.' Only 5 per cent of through-street residents felt the same way.

Zooming in on the people living in the bulb cul-de-sacs, almost 26 per cent strongly agreed that 'a feeling of friendship runs deep between me and my immediate neighbours'. No one on a through street felt that way.

But perhaps the most telling piece of evidence for how much tighter the social fabric is on cul-de-sacs is the fact that when Hochschild was conducting his survey of the 110 homes in Connecticut, somebody called the police to say, 'There is a strange man taking notes about our houses.' It was a resident of a cul-de-sac.

I am not advocating that we build more and more cul-de-sacs, but I am advocating keeping shared spaces in mind when thinking about how we create more connected homes, streets and neighbourhoods.

In 2020, Realdania – a Danish foundation with the mission of improving quality of life through the built environment – published 'Danes in the Built Environment', a study which, among other things, looked into how much interaction neighbours have with each other and how the design of the space they live in plays a part in this. Whereas Hochschild dealt with 110 homes in suburbia, the Realdania study talked to more than 2,300 Danes living in flats.

The study showed that you are almost twice as likely to have a meal with your neighbours if you have a nice common outdoor space. And this community feeling goes beyond food. You are much more likely to help each other out with projects, keep an eye on each other's homes to protect them from burglary, lend things to each other, babysit pets, borrow tools – all those things that make life easier and more hygge if you have good neighbours. But perhaps most importantly, the Realdania study also showed that people who have good relationships with their neighbours experienced a higher level of quality of life.

IMPACT OF SHARED OUTDOOR SPACE ON NEIGHBOUR RELATIONSHIPS

WHICH ACTIVITIES DO YOU TAKE PART IN WITH YOUR NEIGHBOURS?

We have a really good common outdoor space

We have a slightly boring common outdoor space

We don't have a common outdoor space

Keep an eye on each other's homes

41.3%

29%

25.6%

Borrow things from each other (e.g. food and tools)

32%

24.8%

14.6%

Invite each other for meals

12%

7.9%

6.7%

TIP FOR DESIGNING HAPPINESS

how to connect with your neighbours wherever you live

Does this mean that you should aim to live in a cul-de-sac if you want to be happy? No: I think the takeaway here is to be aware of the effects that living on a cul-de-sac, or on a through street or with common spaces will have on you, because we all benefit from feeling part of a community and having good relationships with our neighbours.

If living on a cul-de-sac means that you are likely to walk less, then be aware of that and make a habit of going for a walk after dinner. Perhaps, since you are more likely than average to be friendly with your neighbours, you can offer to walk their dogs once a week. And if you live on a through street, consider what you can do to create a stronger sense of community with your five closest neighbours. Is there a common project you could unite around? Or could you perhaps co-own a lawnmower? If you live in a flat and are having a party, make sure you tell your neighbours that there might be some noise and extend the invitation to them, if it's appropriate, so they can join in the fun. If you live somewhere without immediate neighbours – lucky you! – having someone to keep an eye on your place while you are away is certainly worth its price in pie, so invite a neighbour over and you'll have a new friend in no time.

A hygge home is never lonely, so building up neighbourly connections is essential to make you feel like you belong and that you are safe inside your home, too.

Beyond the home: can architecture and design help integration?

——

Emil puts the key in the door to his new apartment and smiles. 'It is fantastic to be able to move into a brand-new building,' he says, and looks around him. The apartment is 33 square metres and he will be sharing it with one other person. Each has a room of their own, but they share the bathroom and the open-plan kitchen.

The rent is a steal, around £300 per month – around £200 below market value – and in a time when low-income groups, among them students, the elderly and refugees, are being squeezed further and further out of Copenhagen due to increases in rent. So Emil is looking forward to living in Frederiksberg, a small municipality completely engulfed by Copenhagen and known for being posh and leafy with a large park, tree-lined streets, and cafés and boutique shops on every corner.

Emil's new home is something called Venligbolig Plus – Friendly Housing Plus. The project started out as an activist idea to make it possible for Danes to invite refugees into their everyday lives. The aim is to support integration and

friendship. Danish students are buddies to refugees and help them with practical matters and understanding their new country. Forty Danish students will move in with young refugees from countries such as Syria and Eritrea.

The apartment building contains thirty-seven flats and was planned as a small community where students and refugees would live side by side and enrich each other's lives. It's a real-estate project that is trying to facilitate the integration of people into the community. The building offers a shared laundry room, a rooftop terrace for mingling, and the common areas, including the staircases, have been made big enough for the residents to be able to use them for social activities: sitting down, having a coffee and a chat with the neighbours.

The students commit to being a mentor and a buddy for a refugee. Emil has already met the two neighbours he will be a buddy to. 'They seem incredibly nice, and I hope we can become good friends,' he says. 'I can help them with job applications or just talk with them. You learn the language that way if you have Danish friends. That is why this project is genius.'

While these sorts of projects aren't happening in every town or city, they are a great example of how social interaction can affect our levels of happiness within our communities and homes. We know that social support is key to wellbeing. Knowing that we have somebody to rely on in times of need is vital. However, we can also increase our level of wellbeing by offering social support. Studies have shown that people who engage in volunteer work experience higher levels of satisfaction with life, an increased sense of purpose and stronger social relationships. The hygge home is not an island, it is a place that knows it is part of a wider community, and it offers support and warmth to those in need.

THE ARCHITECTURE OF
HAPPINESS CHECKLIST

———

❏ Consider ways in which you can move the cooking or assembling of food from the kitchen to the dinner table to make family dinners last longer.

❏ Apply the vacant chair principle to ensure that nobody feels left out.

❏ Design questions to stimulate meaningful conversations.

❏ Find ways to connect more with your neighbours.

CHAPTER

6

—

WORK HYGGE,
PLAY HYGGE

Not all jobs can be done at home. These days, I am usually tied to a computer, but I have worked as a gardener and as a cleaner in a supermarket, I have sold Christmas trees and tickets in a cinema, I've worked in a botanical garden and I've done night shifts as a baker (Danish pastries, in fact, just to be a cliché). None of those jobs could have been done at home.

In 2020, two things spread globally and rapidly: Covid-19 and remote working. Work that had previously been considered impossible to do remotely moved online within a matter of months, or even weeks.

The good news is that millions of people began to enjoy the benefits that come with remote working. Commutes have been replaced with morning yoga and afternoon walks. Meanwhile, studies show that productivity levels have not dropped.

The benefits have not gone unnoticed by businesses. Some predict that, whatever happens, this might be the end of the nine-to-five job as we know it. Facebook management has said that 50 per cent of its jobs will be remote within ten years, while Twitter has said that its global workforce can continue to work from home. Global law firm Slater and Gordon has given up its London office and other companies are exploring ways in which to rationalize the properties they own or rent and reduce office space by having more employees work flexibly and remotely.

There has been a redefinition of the significance of place, and people are starting to rethink and redesign core elements of their lives too. Remote working will make living further away from companies in the big cities possible. Why not work from the countryside where the house prices are low – or how about Lisbon? I hear the city is lovely at this time of year.

The bad news is that as we move away from the traditional nine-to-five the boundaries between office and home are becoming increasingly blurred. Some studies suggest that many workers don't feel comfortable taking sick leave while working remotely or feel they need to increase their output and working hours to compensate for the lack of visibility offered by an office. Does the afternoon walk mean we burn the midnight oil to reassure our colleagues and bosses we are working hard? Does working remotely mean being remotely happy?

We will also have to adjust the ways in which we share knowledge. We learn from listening to other people's conversations; young team members, in particular, report that they are missing out on both formal and informal incidental learning. The introduction into the company and, with that, the socializing process, is even more challenging. So, where is the virtual water cooler? How do we create team spirit and transfer knowledge seamlessly while working remotely? And do we all need to move into a bigger home so as not to hear the video calls of the people we're living with?

In 2021, management consultancy McKinsey published the results of its research into the future of work in the post-pandemic world. Surveying more than 5,000 employees across Europe, Asia, Australia and North and South America, they found that around 30 per cent of people said that they would be likely to change their job if they had to return to work full time at their place of work. The majority of people (53 per cent) would like to work from home for at least three days a week. I am a fan of the hybrid model myself – days at the office and days working from home. The office allows me to stay connected with my colleagues so we can find solutions together right away, and working from home allows me to focus on more complex tasks – and hang up the laundry when I need a short break.

EMPLOYEE WORKING FROM HOME PREFERENCE

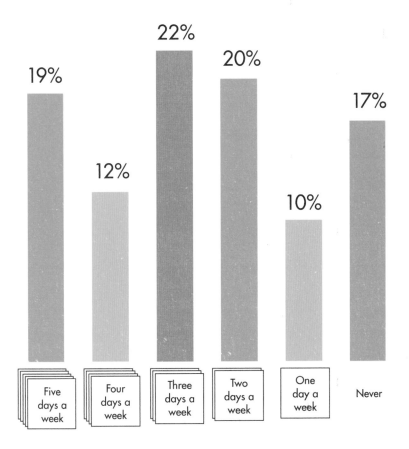

Remote working poses both a risk and an opportunity for our wellbeing. There has never been a more critical time for changes in the workplace. Getting it wrong could lead to an epidemic of burnout. But getting it right could reap huge happiness dividends. So how do we get it right? How do we create good conditions for wellbeing while working remotely?

Six things to keep in mind when designing your workspace

SEPARATE WORK AND PLAY

When the Happiness Research Institute looked into what makes some people more satisfied with their homes than others, one man said he found it beneficial that when working from home he has the ability to draw a curtain around his workstation. That means he can easily mentally shut off after work, simply by drawing the curtain shut. On the other hand, one woman we spoke to said that her workstation was visible at all times in her living room, which means that she is constantly in work mode.

It is important to understand how visible objects trigger our mental capacity. If you can see your workstation, you are going to have a constant reminder of work, so a home office should ideally be a separate space in your home, somewhere you can shut the door or draw a curtain to fulfil the essential need to separate your work life from your home life. Most people don't have a spare room or office – I don't – but perhaps you have a spare bedroom that can function as a dual-purpose space. I don't have a guest room either, so I store my laptop away, out of sight, after I finish working at home. Another good hack is to get a desk that can be folded away at the end of the day so that you get that space back when you've finished and it's not a permanent reminder of work.

USE VIDEO MEETINGS TO GET TO KNOW YOUR WORK TRIBE BETTER

You know those random things you see behind your colleagues on a video call? They often hide great stories and insights, things you might not have known about them had you spoken only in the office. It turns out that Ina's favorite dinosaur is the Ankylosaurus, Alejandro has some mad ice-sculpting skills, and the plant behind Micah is not in fact a real plant. It is made of plastic – which he discovered only after watering it for four months. In turn, Onor's certificate on the wall prompted me to disclose the fact that the only trophy I got after years of playing sports as a kid was the 'Good friend award' – also known as the 'You really suck at sports' trophy.

MAKE SURE YOU SCHEDULE BREAKS

Hygge is about giving your adult overachiever a break, so make sure you make time for breaks when working from home. Fortunately, there is a bakery just around the corner from my house that honestly makes the best cinnamon buns in Copenhagen, so I don't need much convincing to pop in there. If you do find it hard to remind yourself, though, a good way to ensure you take a break is to schedule a call with a friend at a certain time and set yourself a reminder so that there's something to look forward to, then you are duty bound to get up and spend time away from your desk.

INCLUDE COMFY FURNITURE

At the Happiness Research Institute we enjoy having sofas as well as desks. When you need to get acquainted with the latest wellbeing reports it is nice to be able to move away from your desk and on to a sofa. This also applies at home – longer stretches of reading can be made more hygge and enjoyable if there are comfy places to do it in.

APPLY THE HYGGE HOME PRINCIPLES TO YOUR WORKSPACE

You probably won't reach peak productivity lying on your bed, but you don't have to work in a sterile environment either, so make sure your workspace is hygge too. Add plants, make sure you make the most of the daylight and consider the texture of the space. I've put a soft rug under my work desk at home and it gives me a sense of calm when I am facing the avalanche in my inbox.

... EXCEPT THE LIGHTING

Warm, cosy light is, unfortunately, not compatible with staying alert and focused – or awake, for that matter. So, for your work zone, you are allowed a get-out-of-jail card from the hygge police. Feel free to add a white, brighter light.

When it comes to designing a space, there are no right or wrong answers, it's just a case of playing around until something fits. Sometimes a new idea might seem completely counterintuitive, but until you try it out, you'll never know. In fact, trial and error is exactly what we have to thank for making two of the world's greatest cities what they are today. For example, at more than one kilometre long, Strøget in central Copenhagen is one of the most popular and longest pedestrianized shopping streets in Europe. In the early 1960s, there were still cars on Strøget and there was even a discussion about banning cyclists from the street to make more room for them! The proposal to turn it into a car-free zone was controversial, with shopkeepers protesting that it would ruin their businesses. Copenhagen's mayor for planning even received death threats.

In 1962, a six-month trial was agreed upon. It was a huge success, and pedestrianization was made permanent and expanded – and Strøget now has some of the highest property prices in the country. The trial marked the beginning of a major change in the approach of Copenhagen to urban life, with a greater emphasis on pedestrian and bicycle access to the city and a reduction of car use.

About fifty years later, New York also began experimenting with pedestrianization. Cars were banned from the areas of Broadway around Times and Herald squares, turning the area into a car-free zone. The city put out chairs for people to sit on and the experiment was so popular that three months later the trial was made permanent.

TIP FOR DESIGNING HAPPINESS

play around with design

I believe the takeaway here is: Play around. Try it out. Experiment. Especially if you are living with someone who may be – shall we say? – change-resistant. Doing a one-month trial to see what it would be like if, say, we placed the bed up against a different wall or painted the wall a different colour, or moved the table where the kids do their homework closer to the kitchen so you can talk while you cook. You may find that the new set-up changes your behaviour and, ultimately, adds to your happiness.

Make room to play

––––

When I was sixteen I lived on 136 Bradley Street in Goulburn, a small town in New South Wales, Australia. I was an exchange student and stayed, among others, with Steve and Catherine, an amazing couple who I am still in contact with today. In fact, we had a Skype coffee last week. One of the many benefits of staying with Steve and Cath was their dog, Max. Each day when I came home from school I would put 'Great Balls of Fire' on the CD player and Max and I would chase each other around the house. This was our after-school routine and one of the highlights of my day. Still today, when I hear that song, I feel like running around the house.

In our work-obsessed society, play is overlooked and undervalued – even ridiculed, unless it's a 'creative' hobby. It's fine to say that you write or paint in your free time, but running around the house singing 'Great Balls of Fire'? Not so much. It's pointless. But the fact that it is pointless is the point.

Play just for the sake of play is vital to our happiness. To me, the good life – a rich life – includes moments of laughter, joy and play. And I am not alone. According to the LEGO Play Well 2020 study, 98 per cent of children say that playing as a family makes them very happy, and 88 per cent of children say that play helps their parents get to know them better.

And the parents seem to agree with their kids when it comes to the benefits

of play. An overwhelming majority of parents – more than nine out of ten – say that play facilitates communication with their child and builds stronger family bonds.

Thankfully, 95 per cent of parents globally say that play is fundamental to a child's happiness and parents see play as being as important as homework to their child's future success and wellbeing. Furthermore, 95 per cent of parents say that play improves family wellbeing. Interestingly, 91 per cent of children say that play makes their parents very happy.

You are probably familiar with LEGO – perhaps one of the biggest Danish contributions to humankind, in a close race with hygge and Hans Christian Andersen, but did you know that the name LEGO is a shortening of the Danish words LEG GODT, which means 'play well'. During the pandemic, a couple of the activities that kept me sane were LEGO and puzzles. And I wasn't the only one – according to a report from consumer research firm NPD, sales of board games, card games and puzzles grew 228 per cent during the pandemic.

A lot of these activities also allow for face-to-face activities. Sitting side by side facing the TV has its limits – we need actual face-time to connect. Make sure you do family activities where you face each other. If you have teenagers, this can be a particularly good card to play. Parents of teenagers often report that they find it difficult to create the right space for conversations with their kids and find it difficult to encourage them to open up. Analogue play allows you to have different conversations. There is no pressure in terms of eye contact, no awkward silences, no pressure to talk. Whether you talk or don't talk, that is fine, we can just sit here together and work on putting this awesome jigsaw. I am here for you.

A hygge home is a home that understands the value of play. We can use play to connect with others, to harness new skills for self-actualization and to boost self-esteem and gain a sense of accomplishment – which are right up there at the top of Maslow's pyramid of needs, giving us a true feeling of fulfilment. In our next happiness lab experiment I would love it if we could find a way to bottle the sensation of putting in the last piece of a 1,000-piece jigsaw puzzle. That's a feeling like no other. To create a hygge home, it's important to remember to play. Remember: you don't have to stop playing because you grow old; you grow old because you stop playing.

Side note: in the kindergarten I went to the rule was that if you misbehaved you had to sit down and do a puzzle. It had two effects: it helped us kids calm down – and still today I believe that making puzzles is the surest way to maintain my bad-boy image. It's right up there, just short of a leather jacket and a Harley. Give me a 1,000-piece jigsaw and I will show you a rebel without a cause.

TIP FOR DESIGNING HYGGE

analogue play – hygge that creates togetherness

To me, analogue play is a central part of living in a hygge home. One hygge and inexpensive activity is to play Sild i Tønden. In Danish, the phrase 'som sild i en tønde' literally means 'like herring in a barrel'. It means standing, lying or sitting really close together – in English, the game is known as Sardines. It's similar to the classic Hide and Seek, but flipped on its head to make it more hygge.

All players except one stand with their eyes closed and count to twenty or fifty, depending on the size of your home or garden. The one player with their eyes open finds a place to hide. When the group of players has finished counting, the hunt is on. The group splits up and goes searching for the player in hiding. But when the first person finds the one hiding, instead of yelling, 'Found them!' they huddle up together in the hiding place – which is what makes the game more hygge.

When the second person finds the hiding place, they hide there too, and so forth. In the end, all but one person will be cuddled up in the hiding place – packed like 'sild i en tønde'. The last person to find the barrel of herrings hides in the next round. If you have young kids, they'll love this game.

This is great for when there are lots of you at home, but there are also so many ways to play in smaller groups. So make sure that you keep your other options for analogue play such as cards, board games or jigsaw puzzles somewhere visible to give you that mental nudge to pick them over the easy option of Netflix.

Play can foster social connections

——

A few years ago I took part in a workshop in Paris. We started out with a small exercise so that everyone could get to know each other. Each team was given a tangerine, fifty straws and a roll of tape and had fifteen minutes to create something out of the straws and the tape that could support the tangerine. The team with the highest-placed tangerine won. In no time, the room was full of energy, ideas bouncing between the walls, grown men and women laughing and playing.

I forget which team won the challenge – definitely not mine – but I do remember the amount of energy in the room and how big people's smiles were. And also how people who fifteen minutes earlier had been strangers were now standing much closer to one another and talking enthusiastically.

Playing is a great way to get people to loosen up and connect. So, if you are bringing people from different groups together, play might do the trick. For instance, a few years ago, when I was having a grill party for my birthday, I organized a pre-grill event in the form of a small tennis tournament. People who had played a lot teamed up with players who had little experience. The tournament was won by Xavier and Kara – a French–Australian duo – but all the players started the grill party with new connections.

Play and laughter are fantastic social tools. Robert Provine was a professor at the University of Maryland and studied the basis of laughter, hiccuping, yawning and other social behaviours. He found that laughter is thirty times more frequent in groups compared to private settings.

We are more likely to laugh and find jokes funny when we hear other people laughing. This is also why audience laughter or pre-recorded laughter is frequently put on sitcoms, as this increases the chance of inducing laughter from the TV audience. You may also laugh more if you watch a funny movie at the cinema than if you watched it at home on the TV by yourself.

Some believe that laughter pre-dates speech and that it originated as an important way to demonstrate friendliness. It was a way to show that you meant no harm and that you wanted to belong. Still today, laughing can be an important social tool that builds bonds between people. This might also be the reason why laughter sounds less like speech and more like an animal call – as if we are signalling to say that we are friendly.

Laughter can also be contagious. You are more likely to catch laughter from someone else if you know them, but google 'Laughter Chain' and see whether you can get through a video without laughing or smiling.

If you are looking for more help with ways to make people laugh, you might find the work done by humour researcher Richard Wiseman helpful. In 2001, he teamed up with the British Science Association for a scientific search for jokes that make people laugh. Wiseman created the website Laugh Lab and asked people to submit jokes and rate them. Forty thousand jokes were submitted and rated by 350,000 people from 70 countries. The experiment showed that the best jokes tend to be short, for example, 'There were two cows in a field. One said, "Moo." The other one said, "I was going to say that!"'

The study also showed that there are cultural differences in what we find funny. Americans seems to prefer jokes with insults, whereas Europeans prefer surreal jokes, for example:

'A German Shepherd went to the telegram office, took out a blank form, and wrote, "Woof. Woof. Woof. Woof. Woof. Woof. Woof. Woof. Woof."

'The person at the counter examined the form and politely told the dog, "There are only nine words here. You could send another 'Woof' for the same price."

'"But," the dog replied, "that would make no sense at all."'

The point of all this is that I think we should incorporate some play elements when we design our work life, in the way we connect with our colleagues, in taking ourselves less seriously and in how we decorate the workspaces where we spend a huge chunk of our lives. Hygge is all about the atmosphere you create with people, and it can happen anywhere, any time, so don't just reserve it for your home.

Lastly, I would like to point out that I think work can and should be a source of happiness – we all need to feel that there is purpose and meaning in life, structure to our days, and a sense of accomplishment is vital to our wellbeing. But at the same time we also want to design our work life so it allows us to have a life outside work. Getting that balance right is difficult

and demands constant attention, consideration and recalibration. Important tools in this endeavour, I believe, are to make our working lives more hygge and enjoyable by building connections with our colleagues and creating a nice environment, and by improving the quality of our free time and the joy of our play. Work hygge, play hygge.

THE ARCHITECTURE OF
HAPPINESS CHECKLIST

❑ If you work from home, do the best you can to achieve a visual separation between work and play. Keep trying out new set-ups to find the best solution for you.

❑ Play for the sake of play. When was the last time you scheduled in fun? We are used to having a work schedule or an exercise routine, but we must not forget to make time for play and plan to have fun.

❑ Have analogue play opportunities visible to encourage you to get away from your screen and engage with your loved ones face to face.

CHAPTER

7

—

THE CÉZANNE
EFFECT

During the Blitz in the Second World War, the House of Commons Chamber was destroyed by incendiary bombs. So in 1943, the House debated how to rebuild the chamber. Should they rebuild it in a semicircular shape as you see in the US Congress? Or should they rebuild it as it had been, in a confrontational rectangular design, allowing the members of parliament to visibly signal their transfer of allegiance from government to opposition by crossing the floor in plain view? Winston Churchill insisted on rebuilding it as it had been.

'It is easy for an individual to move through those insensible gradations from Left to Right but the act of crossing the Floor is one which requires serious consideration. I am well informed on this matter, for I have accomplished that difficult process, not only once but twice,' he pointed out. He argued that the shape of the old Chamber was responsible for the two-party system, calling it the essence of British parliamentary democracy, and emphasized that 'We shape our buildings and afterwards our buildings shape us.'

In May 1945, the clearance of the site began, and the building was completed five years later – along similar lines to the old building. The adversarial set-up was kept, allowing for intimate and lively debate, including the red lines on the carpet, which are said to be two sword lengths apart and which should not be stepped over during debates.

The building was kept small, containing only 427 seats for 646 members of parliament. Churchill had argued for this. He believed that if the House was big enough to contain all its members, the vast majority of the debates would be conducted in the depressing atmosphere of an almost empty chamber. To him, the essence of good House of Commons speaking was the conversational style and the facility for quick, informal interruptions and interchanges.

I am with Churchill on this one. Having done a lot of public speaking, I know it is much better to have 110 people in an auditorium that seats 100 than 110 people in an auditorium that seats 200.

This is just one example of how our history and identity shine through our surroundings and design choices. The colours we choose, our furniture, the items we display: they all reveal something about us and remind us of who we are.

Our homes are no different to the Houses of Parliament. 'Orrdeerrrr!' Our homes embody how we live and how we see ourselves. That is why a sense of identity and belonging is a key feature of the home. That is what we found when the Happiness Research Institute surveyed more than 13,000 people across Europe. A sense of identity accounts for 17 per cent of the emotions that contribute to how happy we are with our home – the feeling that our home is a place that is an integral part of ourselves, that it tells the story of who we are and where we come from. Our home provides us with a sense of belonging and represents who we are and how we would like the world to see us. Or, as Ellen, a woman in her mid-forties from Amsterdam we interviewed, put it, 'Home is the place where you can be authentic. I feel at home here. Our home has our identity in it. It makes me feel that it is connected to myself.'

We also found that a personal home, one that is strongly linked with your identity, is the home that you are more likely to be proud of, and somewhere you nourish your self-esteem. Maslow placed esteem just above belonging and relationships in the hierarchy of needs – and it is important for our wellbeing.

When we include self-esteem metrics in our studies at the Happiness Research Institute we make good use of the Rosenberg Self-esteem Scale, which asks to what extent you agree with statements such as 'I feel that I have a number of good qualities' and 'I feel I do not have much to be proud of.'

Our home is a collection of our lives. It shows who we are and where we have been. It should help to remind us of our qualities and what we can be proud of. It is a treasure trove of memories and stories about us. A hygge home has personality – it shows people who you are.

If you are like me, you love exploring what other people have on their bookshelves. What are their interests? Have we read some of the same books? Are you into fiction, or how is that third biography of Napoleon different from the other two?

Visiting someone's home is always a great way to get to know someone better, and a hygge home is something that can help us connect with one another and create more meaningful relationships and deeper conversations.

This does not happen overnight. We are twice as likely to strongly agree that our home is designed the right way for how we want to live in it when we are older compared to when we are young, according to IKEAs 'Life at Home' report of 2020 – 49 per cent and 25 per cent respectively. A hygge home is about creating a home that is uniquely yours. Your home is an expression of your identity but, as Churchill pointed out, your home will also shape who you are. It's a two-way street.

IKEA'S 'LIFE AT HOME' REPORT

49%
happiness with home

25%
happiness with home

16–24 YEAR-OLDS   65–75 YEAR-OLDS

The pyramid penthouse

—

As I mentioned earlier, one essential function of our homes is obviously to meet basic needs. They ensure a sense of safety, protection and comfort – the basic level of Maslow's hierarchy of needs. But they can also be used to cover the very top of the hierarchy of needs, self-actualization – the penthouse of the pyramid.

The belief is that our needs form an integrated hierarchy, where our basic needs, such as safety, belonging and self-esteem have to be satisfied – at least to a certain degree – for us to be able to take care of the need for self-actualization higher up in the hierarchy.

Self-actualization can be described as the realization or fulfilment of one's talents and potentialities and can be considered as a drive or need present in everyone. It's to do with becoming who we have the potential and desire to become. A key to happiness.

Self-actualization can easily – and mistakenly – be interpreted as a selfish endeavour, so I think it is important to understand that it also means being socially compassionate and interested and having a sense of oneness with all humanity. How can I use my skills and my talents to serve humanity? According to Maslow, people such as Eleanor Roosevelt and Albert Einstein

are examples of self-actualization. Both have been sources of inspiration for me. For instance, it was Albert Einstein's advice, 'Try not to become a man of success. Rather become a man of value,' that played a large part in me setting up the Happiness Research Institute a decade ago.

But, you might ask, how is self-actualization connected with happiness? That is a great question – well done. Well, Scott Barry Kaufman, a psychologist who teaches wellbeing at Columbia University and the University of Pennsylvania, explored how self-actualization is connected with wellbeing in a 2018 paper.

Surveying more than 500 participants about their level of self-actualization and asking them to say to what extent they agreed with statements such as 'I feel as though I have some important task to fulfil in this lifetime' and 'I accept all of my quirks and desires without shame or apology,' and also looking at a range of indicators of wellbeing, the study found that self-actualization scores are associated with greater life satisfaction, curiosity, self-acceptance, positive relationships, autonomy and purpose in life. Both life satisfaction and purpose in life are key factors when we measure happiness in our studies at the Happiness Research Institute – and autonomy and positive relationships are often found as key drivers of both.

The question then becomes how can our homes help us in working towards self-actualization? It means curating your space so you are reminded of what you love to do and inspires you to do it. Let's take a closer look at how the rooms in our home affect us.

TIP FOR DESIGNING HAPPINESS

check every floor of the pyramid

Consider how your home can help you fulfil the different needs you have. As I've already said, a happy life is not only about surviving and being safe, we also have a need for love, belonging, self-esteem and self-actualization – the higher needs in Maslow's hierarchy.

Our homes are not just a matter of four walls and a roof. A home should give you a sense of both safety and belonging but also help you to connect with other people and to flourish. That is what takes us from surviving to thriving. These things are what makes a house a home. I would argue that our homes can play a role in meeting these needs as well.

PHYSIOLOGICAL NEEDS

Take a moment to appreciate everything that your home supports you with on a basic level. Gratitude is an essential aspect of hygge, and often we have much more around us than we even realize.

SAFETY NEEDS

We all need a sense of shelter and comfort and a hygge home should automatically make your shoulders relax.

SELF-ESTEEM

Place memory triggers around your home to remind you of the things you've done, the things you love, where you've been and how wonderful you are.

LOVE AND BELONGING

The home is considered hygge headquarters. It is where we invite and connect with our nearest and dearest. Having people over to your place can make it easier for them to get to know you and for you all to form a stronger sense of connection.

SELF-ACTUALIZATION

Your behaviour is affected by your surroundings. You can use your home to nudge you towards doing the things that bring you more happiness.

A home away from home

———

My work takes me around the world. In 2019, I spoke in more than thirty cities, from Cape Town in the south and Vancouver in the north to Santiago in the west to Beijing in the east. International travel is less fun and exotic than it sounds. It is mainly waiting in airports and having your circadian rhythm disrupted. But you do get to meet lovely people around the world – and experience first-hand how different spaces impact on your mood and your behaviour, either on a grand scale, like the way Paris just begs of you to sit down and have a coffee and watch the world go by, or on a small scale, for example how the hotel room you are staying in makes you feel.

Let me share two very different experiences with you. One December I was in Beijing for a lecture at Tsinghua University. I had never been to China before and was amazed by the city – I couldn't wait to explore. However, I had the nicest hotel room I had stayed in all year. It wasn't because it was luxurious but because it had been created with care. Someone had thought, what can we do to make this place feel like home for our guest? What they had done was little things – like putting a green plant or two and a small collection of books in the room, books you actually might want to read, or at least flick through. And the place felt like someone's place. It had character. It had personality. Identity. Someone had taken care over it and it felt more like home than any hotel I had stayed in that year. Despite wanting to explore Beijing, it was tempting not to leave the hotel.

That feeling was a stark contrast to an experience I'd had a few months earlier. My colleague and I were in Berlin to meet with one of our clients, and I had booked us a couple of rooms at a hotel near their headquarters in Berlin Mitte. My room had the furniture you would expect in a hotel room. There was a bed, a bedside table, even a small dinner table and four chairs. But there was no soul.

There was a picture frame on the bedside table. In it was the picture that probably came with the frame. A picture of a sheep. It wasn't even a famous sheep. Neither Dolly the clone nor a character from a Haruki Murakami novel. Things had been put into the room – but with no consideration. No thought. No love.

Some places just have a certain something. Whether it's a hotel room, a tiny apartment or a big house, they feel warm and welcoming. My room in Beijing was one of those places. It was like a home away from home. I felt welcomed and relaxed. In Berlin, I felt estranged and in transit.

These experiences led me to ask new kinds of questions about rooms and homes. Instead of considering what a room looks like, I started to ask whether I felt like spending time in it. What would I be likely to do in this space? What kind of behaviour would I like my room to inspire me to? How would the design of the room influence my mood and my behaviour while I was in it?

The setting influences the script. It impacts on our behaviour. Think how differently you act at a football game compared to at a restaurant. However, it wasn't until I later visited Cézanne's studio that I fully understood how spaces can inspire us and, in turn, affect our behaviour.

Cézanne's studio is located on a steep hill on the outskirts of Aix-en-Provence in the south of France. Surrounded by a lush green garden, it is a two-storey yellowish building with red shutters, and the working space upstairs has a huge window facing north and a smaller one facing south. To ensure the best possible light conditions for painting, Cézanne needed daylight, but not direct sunlight. The colour of the paint on the walls and the choice of a wooden floor rather than tiles ensured there was minimal glare.

Next to the north-facing window is what appears to be a giant vertical letterbox in the wall, a curious hole about 30 centimetres wide running from floor to ceiling. It was there so that giant canvases could be brought in and taken out of the studio with ease.

From 1902 until his death in 1906, Cézanne worked here every morning. It was as if he had just popped out when I visited, as his bowler hat and coat are still there, along with easels and the objects he used in his still-life paintings, which you can spot again and again. Fruit bowls, jars, olive pots, a cupid figure, a tablecloth.

Cézanne ordered, according to his own plans, the construction of this studio, and it is evident that the studio is designed with one aim in mind: to create the best possible conditions for painting, and to help him produce the masterpieces that can now be seen in some of the greatest museums in the world. Or, as Abraham Maslow put it, 'A musician must make music, an artist must paint, a poet must write, if he is to be ultimately happy. What a man can be, he must be. This need we may call self-actualization.'

Now, I have never had any talent or interest in drawing or painting. My greatest masterpiece was copying a cover of *Lucky Luke*, my favourite

comic-book series, by tracing it when I was seven. But standing there in Cézanne's studio, the light so perfect, for the first time in my life I wanted to pick up a brush. I wanted to paint.

That is the level of inspiration and motivation the room offered. This was a room that was designed to make you want to paint, to create, to see things as they really are. It was while I was standing in Cézanne's studio that I realized why I had shaped my home office the way I had. I had tried to create a room made for writing.

It's where I've placed my book collection, the American novels I read and the Russian novels I never finished. And the objects that remind me of adventure and exploration: a mask from Indonesia, a lamp from Morocco and my spearfishing equipment. Aides-memoires to my roots: a painting of my grandad's farm, a camera from the 1960s he gave to my dad, a stool I made with my uncle from a branch of a hundred-year-old cherry tree. Every object triggers memories, and this is the reservoir of stories and experiences I tap into as I write.

There is a collection of Korean masks given to me by a young man who lost his mother to suicide and now fights against the social stigma around mental illness in Korea; he wants to encourage us to remove the masks that we all wear. To me it is a reminder of a global collective effort in trying to make the world a better place.

In my last book, I joked about the fact that the hotel I always stay in in London has a replica of Leonardo da Vinci's *Lady with an Ermine* in every room. After the book was published, my team at Penguin Random House sent me a copy of the painting and it hangs in my home office.

228

There is the chair I bought myself to have a physical memento of the accomplishment I felt for having my first book published. There is a daybed for reading, as my first step in writing is studying. And finally, there is the desk, a beautiful one in walnut with a black linoleum top. A desk that begs you to sit down and write.

I know this is a not so subtle and not so humble bit, saying, 'Yeah, me and Cézanne, we are totally on the same page. Buddy buddies. Creative geniuses.' What the world needs is surely more humble geniuses – there are so few of us left.

Joking aside, I believe the lesson here is that rooms and homes can inspire us. Motivate us to become who we strive to be. Housing is not a noun, it is a verb – or it should be. It is how building and designing continuously allow us to flourish. A happy home can help us pursue our passions and become who we want to become. That is the Cézanne effect – when a home inspires us, when it facilitates self-actualization. Echoing the words of Churchill, we shape our buildings and then they shape us.

Let's look at two examples of how our homes shape us, both physically and intellectually.

Shelf-development

——

Let me ask you a question. How many books were in your home when you were sixteen? One metre of books on the shelves is equivalent to around forty books. The answer in my case is around 350 books.

The reason I ask is that it is an example of how spaces can shape us without us knowing about it. One study by a group of researchers from Australian National University asked that exact question and examined data from more than 160,000 people from thirty-one countries, combined with information on their levels of literacy and numeracy.

Yes, the average number of books varies a lot from country to country, from 27 in Turkey to 218 in Estonia. And yes, the education level of your parents, what they do, and how much they read are predictors of your literacy level – but so is the number of books in your home when you were a teenager, even when we control for other factors.

COUNTRY – AVERAGE
NUMBER OF BOOKS

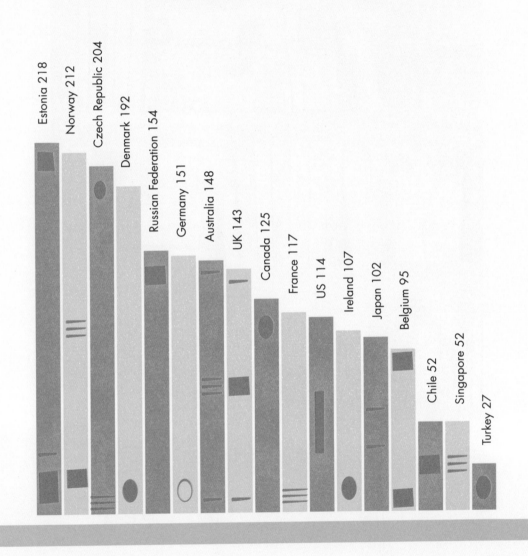

Estonia 218

Norway 212

Czech Republic 204

Denmark 192

Russian Federation 154

Germany 151

Australia 148

UK 143

Canada 125

France 117

US 114

Ireland 107

Japan 102

Belgium 95

Chile 52

Singapore 52

Turkey 27

The study showed that a sixteen-year-old with no books at home went on to have below-average levels for literacy and numeracy, whereas teenagers with only lower levels of secondary education but from a book-stacked home 'become as literate, numerate and technologically apt in adulthood as university graduates who grew up with only a few books'.

So, if your child walks into a library and says, 'Two cheeseburgers, please,' and the librarian replies, 'This is a library,' and your child repeats in a whisper, 'Sorry – two cheeseburgers, please,' you need to put more books in your home. In short, get your kids familiar with books. And don't worry – you don't need an entire library. According to the study, around 80 books raises literacy levels to the average, and having above 350 books is not associated with any additional effect. Of course, eighty books is a lot, so you may want to get to know your local second-hand bookshop.

You might say, 'I don't care about books and reading.' OK, fine. Three things. First, I am sorry that we can't be friends any more. Second, the point is that your home and your room impact on you and your behaviour. You act differently in different room settings, so simply having books there will make a difference. And finally, keep in mind that Cicero, the Roman statesman and scholar, is said to have pointed out that a home without books is like a body without a soul. What he meant was of course that a home without books lacks hygge. A modern variation is John Samuel Waters Jr, an American actor and director, who is credited with saying, 'If you go home with somebody and they don't have books, don't sleep with them.' Don't sleep with people who don't read. A variation of that could be: No books equals no hygge.

However, books are just one example of how we first shape our homes and then they shape us. One study from University College London used data from more than 12,000 children born around the turn of the century who were part of the UK Millennium cohort study and thus followed over time to understand how conditions in childhood affect adult life.

At the age of seven, around 50 per cent of the kids had a TV in their bedroom, and four years later these kids were 20 per cent more likely to become overweight if they were boys, and 30 per cent more likely if they were girls.

According to lead author Dr Anja Heilmann from the University College London Institute of Epidemiology and Health Care, there is a clear link between having a TV in the bedroom as a kid and being overweight a few years later. She believes that childhood obesity prevention strategies should consider access to TVs in children's bedrooms as a risk factor for obesity.

I've been subject to this effect as well. When I was a kid, we would spend the summers in our summer cabin with one 14-inch black-and-white television with a bad aerial connection. Subsequently, we watched a lot less television. During the summer of 1992 – I was fourteen – the only thing I watched on TV was the final of the European Championship in football when Denmark played Germany – and won! Since then, our screens have become flatter, but our kids have become wider. In other words, how we design our children's rooms – and our own – can directly impact on our health and our wellbeing.

TIP FOR DESIGNING HAPPINESS

think function first

Consider how different furniture will impact on what takes place in the room. Instead of filling the empty room with what might be standard for a room – a light on the ceiling, paintings or posters on the wall, chairs or a sofa – start with what you would like that room to give you. It is a more humanistic approach that puts you as a person at the core of the space. If you're not sure, ask yourself these questions:

- What function would you like the room to have in your life?
- What need or what desire are you hoping to find solutions for?
- Is this a room for socializing or for comforting time alone?
- What do you need to be comfortable here?

If your home or room is small, you may have to prioritize which functions are the most important to you and so which should take up more space. Is your perfect night in a dinner party with your friends or spending all day watching *The Lord of the Rings*? Answering this may help you decide whether your dinner table or your sofa should be allocated the larger space.

If you love to paint, allow your space to remind you of that. We can't all afford to build a studio from the ground up with perfect lighting and a giant vertical letterbox for our huge canvases like Cézanne, but perhaps we could have an easel. Perhaps we could include some of the elements that Cézanne used for his still lifes. An empty wine bottle, a jug of water, a bowl of fruit. The skull – perhaps not.

A hygge home means a series of spaces that remind you of who you are and what brings you happiness. It means making space for what you love to do.

Beyond the home – finding home when our memory is fading

———

Identity is also key when we are struggling with finding our way home. Having a unique front door can help people navigate in a difficult world.

In the Pieter van Foreest Weidevogelhof care facility in Pijnacker – a small town between Rotterdam and the Haag in the Netherlands – all the doors were the same colour, an institutional orange with a blue frame. For people living with dementia, moving into a new home, often in the form of an assisted-living facility, can be frightening. Where am I? Where is home? However, one Dutch company came up with a simple solution to make the transition a bit easier and the new place feel a bit more like home. They thought, why don't we make the resident's new door look like the door they are used to? One door might be made to look like it was beautiful carved wood, another would appear to have coloured glass mosaics and one as if it has graffiti on it. Perhaps this last resident lived in a big city and misses the urban atmosphere.

A photo is taken of the old front door – perhaps a door that has been the symbol of home for fifty years – printed out and put on the door that leads

237

into their new room. If a photo cannot be taken, there is a catalogue with hundreds of options where people can find something that resembles what they had.

This makes it easier for people to find their room and makes it less likely for them to walk into the wrong room. But, most importantly, it takes a clinical and impersonal atmosphere, which can often be found in assisted-living facilities, and gives it a more homely and friendly feeling. While we may lose what have been our homes for decades, we never lose our need for a sense of belonging.

THE ARCHITECTURE OF
HAPPINESS CHECKLIST

———

❑ Think about how your home fulfils all your needs, from the basics of safety and functionality to supporting your relationships, all the way through to affirming your sense of identity and, ultimately, self-actualization.

❑ Put your own stamp on it. Whether you own or rent, make sure it feels like your place. It is all about feeling that your home expresses who you are.

❑ Think function first, rather than focusing on what it looks like. How does your space make you feel and do things? Be mindful of the consequences of your design choices. Are the chairs and sofas positioned for TV bingeing or for conversation? How much of a house altar is the TV? Can it be in a cabinet so you can shut the cabinet doors and hide it when you're not watching it?

❑ Use the decor to inspire action. If your grandpa's old typewriter reminds you of how he taught you to read, keep it on a bookshelf or by your desk.

CHAPTER

8

—

HYGGE IS
HOME-MADE

Last autumn, my friend Mikkel and I took a beer-brewing course together. That afternoon, after four fun hours of playing with hops, malt and yeast, I cycled home with sixteen litres of IPA brew on the back of my bike.

But that was just the beginning of the beer-making process. For the next couple of weeks, the yeast would eat the sugar, creating carbon dioxide and alcohol. In other words, that is where the magic and the hygge happen. The beer was kept in a fermenter with an airlock so the carbon dioxide could escape, making the sound of bubbly hygge. I kept the fermenter in my home office, but the smell of IPA forced me to use other parts of the apartment to work in. A short-term sacrifice for long-term hygge. After the fermentation process was complete, it was time to bottle the beer and then store it for a few more weeks to make sure the taste had developed. It was a long wait and a lot of work, but hygge all the way. I named it the Little Brew of Hygge.

If you have read *The Little Book of Hygge*, you may remember that I also attempted to make limoncello – with the same result in terms of hygge. My next project is going to be cider. I am aware that the common denominator is alcohol, but it doesn't have to be. I believe that one key to hygge is the home-made element. There is something soothing about having to monitor the development of whatever is cooking or brewing or fermenting. You could say that fermentation is the extreme sport of hygge slow food.

It is said that the recipe for happiness includes something to do and something to look forward to. So pick a food project that will run for a couple of months. It might be kimchi or cider or, if you just want to start with something really simple, how about preserved lemons? They are super-easy and taste and look amazing.

TIP FOR DESIGNING HAPPINESS

preserved lemon recipe

This process will transform the lemons, removing the bitterness from them and creating an intense, concentrated lemon flavour. You'll only need a little for a big flavour hit. Preserved lemons are basically lemons on steroids.

1. Find an old jam jar and clean it out. You can sterilize it by boiling it, but be careful. Scalding yourself is not hygge.

2. Squeeze the juice from one or two lemons.

3. Wash and quarter several lemons, but don't cut all the way through – the four quarters should hold together at one end.

4. Rub a generous dose of salt into each lemon, then place them in the jar, squeezing them together.

5. Put another generous dose of salt in the jar, and the juice of the lemons, making sure all the lemons are coated.

6. Store the jar in the fridge or in a cool cupboard away from direct sunlight, for one month or, preferably, two.

7. Go crazy with lamb casseroles and Moroccan salads!

Hygge food is really about how to get the best flavour out of simple ingredients. And sometimes, one of the vital ingredients is time. Cooking at home is not only cheaper and healthier, it also provides something vital for our happiness – the sense of accomplishment and satisfaction that comes from putting a dish on the table that you have created. But, most importantly, cooking is an act of love. It is a way to show people that you care, that you prepared and created something for them to enjoy. That is why hygge happens in the kitchen. You might know this from house parties, where the best part of the party often takes place in the kitchen.

That is why I loved seeing the results from a recent survey commissioned by Anglian Home Improvements of 1,000 UK homeowners that looked into exactly what makes a house a home. What is it that takes walls and bricks and turns it into our own little paradise? I think it is interesting to see that no physical stuff made it into the top five. The first item is the sofa, in seventh place – but love, the sound of laughter and family meals are the heavyweights when it comes to making a home.

WHAT MAKES
A HOUSE A HOME?

Happiness	57%
Love	51%
Security and safety	50%
The sound of laughter	44%
Meals with family and friends	43%
The smell of good food cooking	43%
A comfy sofa	42%
A bath *and* a shower	40%
Freshly laundered sheets each week	39%
A well-stocked fridge	39%
Framed pictures of family and friends	39%
Pets	36%
Children	32%
Sunday roasts	32%
Summer BBQs in the garden	32%
Your collections – e.g. books, paintings and DVDs	31%
Having a place just for you in your house	30%
Festive celebrations	25%
Comfy corners	25%
Good cushions	23%
An open fire in the winter	22%
Candles	22%
Holiday pictures	20%

Madglæde

One of my favourite photographs was taken in the Maine woods in 1894. It shows a group of ten men and women in their best clothes and big hats enjoying an outing, each of them holding up a slice of watermelon so that it looks like they each have an oversized grin on their face. While their mouths might be hidden by the watermelon, their eyes show how happy they are. This is just one photograph, but the evidence of the relationship between food and happiness is everywhere. Across time and space, food is perhaps one of the most basic sources of happiness.

English philosopher Jeremy Bentham (1748–1832) was one of the first to try to quantify happiness. According to Bentham, people act to maximize pleasure and minimize pain and he formulated the Hedonic Calculus, which is used to calculate how much pleasure or pain an action will generate. Happiness is often associated with hedonism and with the Greek philosopher Epicurus, who believed that the presence of pleasure and the lack of pain would lead to complete happiness. Another school of thought comes from the Greek philosopher Aristotle, who believed that the good life and happiness are achieved through living a meaningful life and by doing virtuous acts. We can trace today's perception of happiness back to both these schools of thought. To me, the good life includes both elements – purpose *and* pleasure.

Including both elements is the best way, I believe, to ensure a good, rich, fulfilling life. A hygge home is therefore also a home that understands madglæde – a Danish word meaning the joy of food or the enjoyment of food. However, recently we have become suspicious of food that provides us with joy. It is almost as if we have to feel guilty about enjoying food, that eating delicious food is a sin.

But hygge is about simple pleasures, like the taste of freshly baked home-made bread and the smell of a bag of coffee beans you've just opened (am I the only one who takes a good whiff of that?). What if we counted the enjoyment and pleasure we get from food as carefully as we count the calories? I am sure Bentham would be on my side on that one. I think we need to redesign the perception of food. If health is not just the absence of disease but full physical, mental and social wellbeing, then healthy food is something that makes us happy, gives us comfort and pleasure and connects us with other people.

Health should also be about pleasure, wellbeing and quality of life. Or, as American food writer Mary Frances Kennedy Fisher puts it in her 1954 classic *The Art of Eating*, 'With good friends . . . and good food on the board . . . we may well ask, when shall we live if not now?'

Hygge is about celebrating life at home, enjoying comfort and pleasure. It's about madglæde. And I believe that right there with madglæde comes an interest in ingredients – and perhaps a desire to start growing them ourselves.

Home-grown hygge

When we did the study about what it is that makes a house a home, we also asked what the participants' ideal home would look like, and several people stated that they dreamed of having a place where they could grow their own fruit and vegetables. One person who did grow their own fruit and vegetables said, 'I think it is a crazy world out there, but we grow our own food here, because we are attempting to be self-sufficient. To me, it represents a place of safety. It is like an ark.'

Another participant – Stefan, who's in his thirties and lives in Berkshire – wrote to us after the interview: 'I have thought of something I wanted to say while we were on the call, but the conversation moved on. It was under the topic of an ideal home – I would very much like to have a vegetable patch or an allotment with a greenhouse or two in the garden, so I could grow vegetables and fruits. Not only is it very enjoyable, healthy, practical and therapeutic, but it also goes back to what we were saying about this desire I think we have to be self-sufficient and provide for one's family.'

So it turns out I am not alone in dreaming about a small plot of land to grow my own vegetables. So far, my biggest yield has been from a small chilli plant on the windowsill, but I have enjoyed every single development. Watching it grow from a flower into a small fruit. Watching it turn from green

to red. Watching it go into my tacos. I think the same thing applies with growing your own vegetables as with cooking your own food. There is a sense of accomplishment and joy that comes from something developing into pure goodness. The next addition to my small home farm is going to be oyster mushrooms, which grow in used coffee grounds.

TIP FOR DESIGNING HAPPINESS

grow something on your windowsill

I know we can't all have a garden – I've lived in an apartment for most of my life – but from plots to pots, there are lots of easy-to-grow vegetables that suit gardens of every size, so don't worry if you don't have a big outdoor space to grow your own food in, a windowsill will get you started. The easiest things to grow are:

1. Radishes, which add crunch and a peppery deliciousness to salads.

2. Spinach, which is delicious wilted through stews or curries, and adds more plants.

3. Microgreens add freshness and colour to the top of any dish.

4. Chilli plants in the window can spice up your life.

5. Tomato plants grow so quickly you can almost watch them growing. If you have kids, this might be the plant to start with.

6. Cucumbers – go for the smaller variant and put in a string above them, as the plant needs something to grow up.

7. Strawberries – and since you are growing them indoors, you don't have to fight with the birds over the sweet berries.

8. Basil – step one in making your home-made pesto for the pantry.

9. Ginger. Cover it with 1–2 centimetres of soil; it doesn't even need direct sunlight – it just likes to be warm and cosy.

10. Parsley, sage, rosemary and thyme. Time to go full Simon and Garfunkel.

Seeds of comfort

———

Prior to opening the Happiness Museum in Copenhagen, we created a contest in which people could nominate objects that symbolized happiness to them. We were overwhelmed by the number of responses we got and how ready people were to donate things to the museum – asthma inhalers, wedding-cake decorations, marathon medals and tomato seeds. The seeds were sent to us by Katie, who lives in the US.

When Katie's father died in 2006, she couldn't bear to throw away his old shirts, so she kept them, taking them with her when she and her family moved. As the ten-year anniversary of her father's death approached, Katie decided to turn the shirts into quilts for her mother and siblings. Going through them, she found an old sticker, some pocket lint, and then, clinging to the cotton, a couple of seeds. Her father had been a keen gardener and she decided to plant the ten-year-old seeds. A few days later, a little green shoot appeared. She watered it and fed it liquid fertilizer and watched the seeds turn into a three-metre-tall tomato plant in her laundry room.

This inspired Katie to become a seed saver and a gardener. From this first plant, she saved some seeds, dried and stored them and planted them out in her garden the following year. Later, she started to share the seeds with friends who had lost loved ones. The idea grew, and she now helps out in a grief camp for children under the name Comfort Seeds.

Kolonihaver – harvesting the hygge

——

As well as my footsteps on the gravel road, I can hear birds chirping and, in the distance, someone digging in the soil. In the air you can smell elderflowers and that someone nearby is baking an apple tart.

I am in one of the many kolonihaver in and around Copenhagen, small garden allotments with colourful wooden houses where the people of Copenhagen can come to get some air into their lungs and some dirt under their fingernails. *Kolonihaver* literally means 'colony gardens', and they are basically a hygge smoothie of slow and simple outdoor living.

The allotments cannot exceed more than 400 square metres and you are not allowed to live in the houses all the year round, usually only from April to October. It would be too cold, anyway, the rest of the year – the homes are small and rarely have good insulation.

Colony gardens began as vegetable gardens and as recreational spots for working-class families in the denser cities in Denmark. They were sometimes referred to as poor man's gardens – it was a way for poorer families to get fresh fruit and vegetables on the table. Today, kolonihaver homes rate high on the hygge scale and if you get to own one you feel rich. Some of the houses are less than 20 square metres, so they are tiny homes but big on hygge, taking simple living to a new level.

I strike up a conversation with the man digging the soil. He and his wife own a bigger flat in central Copenhagen but spend at least four months here every summer with their small son. 'We are together in a different way here,' he explains. 'We are just together, being outside, feeling good. You know, hygge.'

They grow fifteen different vegetables on their plot, which also has a couple of apple trees. He said, 'I work in IT and I enjoy that, but there is nothing as satisfying as growing your own vegetables.'

TIP FOR DESIGNING HAPPINESS

---

there is nothing hygge about wasting food

A recent report showed that UK households waste 4.5 million tonnes of food a year or, to put it in monetary terms, £14 billion worth – that's £700 for the average family with kids each year. And the level of waste is even worse in the US: several studies have shown that American households waste between 30 and 40 per cent of their food. According to the *American Journal of Agricultural Economics*, the average American household wastes food worth $1,866 a year. In addition, food waste is responsible for 6–8 per cent of global greenhouse-gas emissions. But the good news is that there is a lot we can do to reduce waste through the way we design our behaviour in the kitchen.

- Have a 'retirement shelf' in your fridge. This is where you place the food that needs to be eaten soon, food that doesn't have many days left before it goes off. This makes it easier for you to be aware of what you have to work into your meals that day or the next.

- Become familiar with catch-all recipes. Do you have some tomatoes, two lumps of cheese, an onion, half a courgette, an almost empty jar of olives, some leftover meat? Good news – it's pizza night! Think soups, risottos, ragouts and casseroles to soak up your leftovers into new meals.

- Berries and other fruit that is going bad can be turned into jam or put in cakes. Apples, rhubarb or oranges? Melt some sugar in an ovenproof pan, add butter and then the fruit. Let it simmer for a few minutes. Take the pan off the heat and let it cool for a few minutes then cover the fruit with some puff pastry and tuck it down the sides (be careful, as the sugar may still be hot). Prick the pastry with a fork and bake in a preheated oven at 200°C for twenty-five minutes. Allow to cool for ten minutes then put a plate on top of the pan and flip it – and your tarte tatin (if you're using apples) is ready for an afternoon of pure hygge.

- Do you have lots of leftover food after a party? Make doggy bags for the guests or, better yet, once a year, host a party where everybody has to bring a dish – but here is the kicker: it has to be a dish based on leftovers or food you already had in the fridge. I'm sure you'll be delighted not just with the taste but also by your friends' creativity.

THE ARCHITECTURE OF
HAPPINESS CHECKLIST

———

❑ Slow food. Whether it is IPA or preserved lemons, make sure you have something to look forward to.

❑ Grow seeds of joy. Chillies or tomatoes, pots or plots, it doesn't matter. Hygge will be the harvest.

❑ Add madglæde. What is your favourite dish? Allow yourself time to cook it at home once a month.

CONCLUSION

———

A HEALING
PLACE FOR THE
SOUL

In one of my earlier books, *The Little Book of Lykke*, I briefly touched upon bibliotherapy, the method of using books to aid people in solving the issues they are facing by reading about characters who are facing similar problems. My belief in the healing power of words has increased still more since then, and one reason for this is the experiences of William Sieghart.

A couple of years ago, I spoke at an event organized by the *Idler* magazine in London. One of the other speakers was William, who believes that poems have the power to restore and heal and has been on a mission to 'get poetry out of poetry corner'.

'I was eight years old when I was first sent to boarding school, as part of that strange British tradition of sending your kids to the other side of the country to a place where no one loves them,' he said. 'I was small and I was lonely and I was scared. I was desperately unhappy. At a time when friends were in short supply, I found that poetry became my friend.'

For the past few years, William Sieghart has listened to the problems of over a thousand people across Britain and given them a curated poem to reduce their burdens. He calls it 'poetry pharmacy'.

What he found is that no matter where you live, we all have the same problems and in fact it is a rather small sample of issues and anxieties that we face – and these are what he has tried to find poetry prescriptions for. And the biggest anxiety of them all? Loneliness. For this, William prescribes a very short poem written in the fourteenth century by the Persian poet Hafiz: 'I wish I could show you when you are lonely or in darkness the astonishing light of your own being.'

The magic potion of poetry shows us that someone, somewhere, has felt what we are feeling now. Someone has distilled the essence of an emotion we thought we alone carried but which in fact we share with all our fellow human beings. Poetry is a way of holding hands with each other, a way of connecting with humanity. A way of understanding how much you have in common with a Persian poet who lived seven hundred years ago – and something that makes you suddenly feel a little less alone in the world. And if you travelled even further back in time, to ancient Greece, and visited the library of Thebes, you would find this inscription above its doors: 'A healing place for the soul'.

My hope is not only that libraries will be healing places for the soul but that our homes can be too. And, furthermore, that we not only use past Persian poetry to aid loneliness but that in the future we design for connection and belonging. That while we are taking poetry out of the poetry corner, we take design out of the pretty things corner.

Every two years, I follow the results of the biennial Index Award initiated by the Danish non-profit organization the Index Project. Its mission is expressed in its motto, 'Design to improve life', and the award is one of the world's biggest in design awards – it has been dubbed the Nobel Prize of Design.

The prize is 500,000 euro and five winners are picked from the hundreds of nominations within five categories: Body, Home, Work, Play and Learning, and Community.

Previous winners include LifeStraw, a plastic straw that cleans contaminated water to prevent diseases such as cholera and typhoid from spreading through drinking water; Street Swags, a bed in a bag designed to provide people living on the street some comfort, warmth and protection from the weather; Sky Greens, an urban vertical farming system that alleviates the environmental impact of farming; and Hövding, an airbag for cyclists that is worn around the neck like a collar. If there's an accident, the airbag is released and protects your head before you hit the ground. Remember, this is Denmark – if you design something for a bike, you get a prize. But these are examples of how design encompasses more than just aesthetically pleasing things.

Design should be about creating solutions for people, about imagining a different – and better – world and creating a plan for how to make that happen. And that includes the spaces we spend more time in than anywhere else – our homes.

This book is not intended to be a to-do list but as a catalogue, or menu, for inspiration. My hope is that you will be more conscious of how our environment impacts on not only our physical but our mental wellbeing and reflect on how our homes can play a part in how we feel. I hope you will take control over how to design, shape and maintain the environments you live and work in so that you can flourish in them.

Currently, roughly a third of all people in the UK say that they occupy a house – not a home. I believe there are ways we can change this by designing spaces and places that bring us joy. I believe we can use hygge to turn our house into a home, into a place that has been designed for connection and for belonging, a place where we find joy and comfort in watching plants grow.

We can utilize the idea of hygge to transform our living and working spaces into places where we count our wealth by the depth of our bonds and the absence of our wants. By the tools we share with our neighbours and by the daylight that lights up our lives. By the quality of our children's play and by the spiciness of our chillies.

And, most importantly, to create a space that encourages us to find time to do what matters most. That allows us to live large on a small budget. That allows us to discover that happiness is best home-made.

PICTURE CREDITS

ACKNOWLEDGEMENTS

So many homes have opened their doors to me over the years and have shaped my view of what makes a hygge home.

I would like to thank the place where we dug tunnels in the back yard; the place where George the Lizard lived under the stairs; the place that had a kitchen big enough to fit in a seven-person TV crew; the place that offered a mattress to crash on; the place where we can always open another bottle of wine; the place where the mistletoe still flies; the place where Dogget spotted the snake; the place where the Mexican train is played; the place that always toasts to sparkling minds and firm bottoms; the place where I always look forward to dinner; the place where croquet is won or lost; the place where you stand for the Queen's Christmas Day speech; the place where we solved the Parisian puzzle; the place where you could always borrow a comic book; the place that plays Irish folk music; the place that always smells of wood; the place where the host had learned all our names; the place where the best band in Latvia resides; the place where there is always a coffee with my name on it; the place where we never made it through *American Pie*; the place where he would sit down so his wife could reach him with a kiss; the place where an afternoon of crosswords is as hectic as it gets; the place where the cards are dealt and the whisky is poured; the place where 'Great Balls of Fire' will always play; and, lastly, to the home of the penguins. Without you all, these books would have been trapped in a drawer.

MEIK WIKING founded the world's first Happiness Research Institute in 2013, in Copenhagen, Denmark. He is the author of three globally bestselling books which have sold over 2 million copies worldwide: *The Little Book of Hygge*, *The Little Book of Lykke* and *The Art of Making Memories*.

 @Happi_Research   @meikwiking